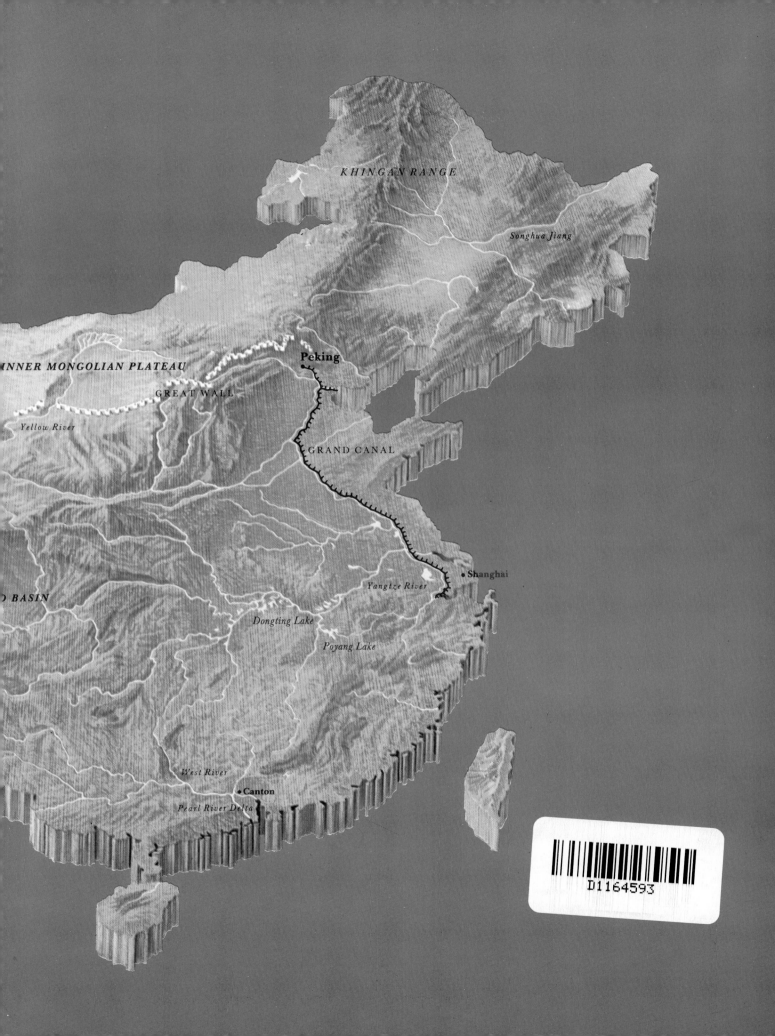

KHINGAN RANGE

Songhua Jiang

INNER MONGOLIAN PLATEAU

GREAT WALL

Peking

Yellow River

GRAND CANAL

BASIN

Shanghai

Yangtze River

Dongting Lake

Poyang Lake

West River

Canton

Pearl River Delta

CHINA

CHINA

By the Editors of Time-Life Books

TIME-LIFE BOOKS · AMSTERDAM

A CHILD'S FIRST LIBRARY OF LEARNING
VOYAGE THROUGH THE UNIVERSE
MYSTERIES OF THE UNKNOWN
TIME-LIFE HISTORY OF THE WORLD
FITNESS, HEALTH & NUTRITION
HEALTHY HOME COOKING
UNDERSTANDING COMPUTERS
THE ENCHANTED WORLD
LIBRARY OF NATIONS
HOME REPAIR AND IMPROVEMENT
CLASSICS OF EXPLORATION
PLANET EARTH
PEOPLES OF THE WILD
THE EPIC OF FLIGHT
THE SEAFARERS
WORLD WAR II
THE GOOD COOK
THE TIME-LIFE ENCYCLOPAEDIA
OF GARDENING
THE GREAT CITIES
THE OLD WEST
THE WORLD'S WILD PLACES
LIFE LIBRARY OF PHOTOGRAPHY
TIME-LIFE LIBRARY OF ART
GREAT AGES OF MAN
LIFE SCIENCE LIBRARY
LIFE NATURE LIBRARY

TIME-LIFE BOOKS

EUROPEAN EDITOR: Ellen Phillips
Design Director: Ed Skyner
Director of Editorial Resources: Gillian Moore
Chief Sub-Editor: Ilse Gray
Assistant Design Director: Mary Staples

LIBRARY OF NATIONS

EDITOR: Martin Mann
Deputy Editor: Phyllis K. Wise
Designer: Raymond Ripper

Editorial Staff for *China*
Associate Editors: Betsy Frankel, David S. Thomson
(text), Jane Speicher Jordan (pictures)
Staff Writer: Thomas H. Flaherty Jr.
Researchers: Denise Li (principal), Scarlet Cheng, Rita
Thievon Mullin, Paula York-Soderlund
Art Co-ordinator: Anne B. Landry
Assistant Designer: Lynne Brown
Sub-Editor: Sally Rowland
Copy Co-ordinators: Margery duMond, Victoria Lee
Art Assistant: Robert K. Herndon
Picture Co-ordinator: Eric Godwin
Editorial Assistant: Cathy A. Sharpe

Special Contributors: The chapter texts were written by:
Oliver Allen, Ronald Bailey, John Cottrell, Donald
Jackson, Keith Wheeler, A. B. C. Whipple and Edmund
White. *Other Contributors:* C. Tyler Mathisen, Lydia
Preston, Fay Willey.

EDITORIAL PRODUCTION FOR THE SERIES
Chief: Ellen Brush
Traffic Co-ordinators: Stephanie Lee, Jane Lillicrap
Editorial Department: Theresa John, Debra Lelliott,
Sylvia Osborne

Correspondents: Elisabeth Kraemer (Bonn); Margot
Hapgood, Dorothy Bacon (London); Miriam Hsia, Lucy
T. Voulgaris (New York); Maria Vincenza Aloisi,
Josephine du Brusle (Paris); Ann Natanson (Rome).

CONSULTANT

Dr. Richard Bush, recipient of a Fulbright-
Hays Fellowship, has done extensive
research in China. Deputy Director of the
China Council of the Asia Society in
Washington D.C., he is author and co-
author of numerous books and articles
on China.

**Cover: Fishing junks moored to the banks
of the Lu River float below wooded
mountain peaks near the town of Guilin in
southern China. The limestone pinnacles,
compared by a Chinese poet to "blue jade
hairpins", are pitted with caves formed by
the action of underground rivers.**

**China's official emblem is shown on page 1;
the building depicted is in Tiananmen Square
in Peking. The national flag is shown on page 2.**

This volume is one in a series of books describing
countries of the world, their lands, peoples, histories,
economies and governments.

Revised 1990
Revision Editor: Windsor Charlton
Sub-Editor: Tim Cooke
Consultant: Ken Campbell
D.L.TO:1527-1990

CONTENTS

Bathers crowd the beach at Qingdao, Shandong province. China's population passed the billion mark in late 1981.

THE MOST POPULOUS NATION

TOTAL POPULATION (MILLIONS)

Although stringent birth-control measures have lowered the birth rate in China, one Chinese child is born every two seconds. The long-term pattern of expanding population *(above)* was interrupted from 1960 to 1962, when famine struck the country in the wake of the Great Leap Forward *(Chapter 5)*; that decline is mirrored below in birth and death records.

MILLIONS   ■ BIRTHS   ■ DEATHS

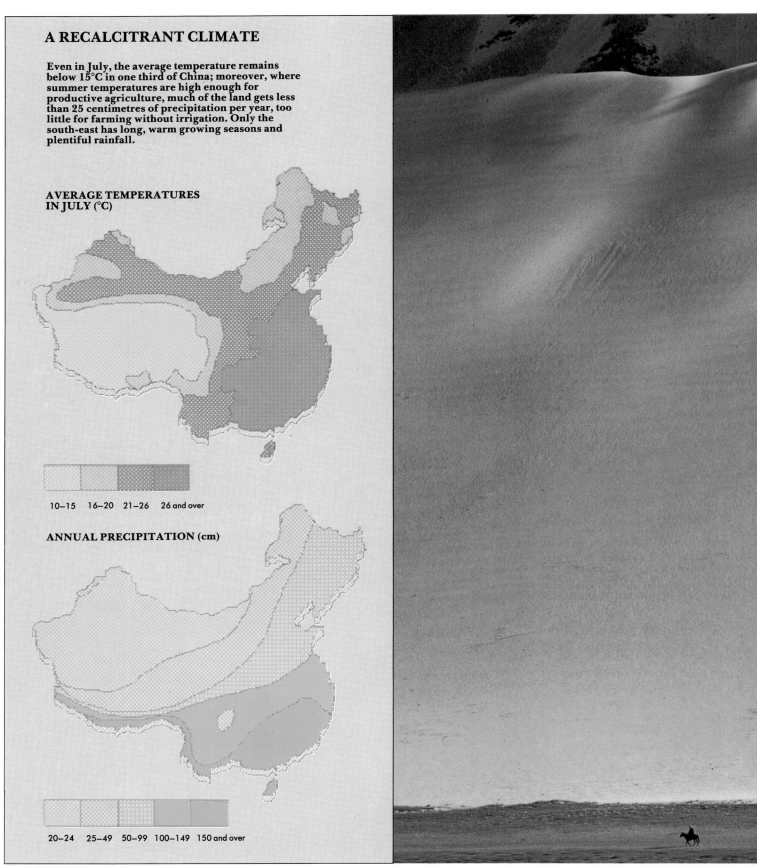

A RECALCITRANT CLIMATE

Even in July, the average temperature remains
below 15°C in one third of China; moreover, where
summer temperatures are high enough for
productive agriculture, much of the land gets less
than 25 centimetres of precipitation per year, too
little for farming without irrigation. Only the
south-east has long, warm growing seasons and
plentiful rainfall.

**AVERAGE TEMPERATURES
IN JULY (°C)**

10–15   16–20   21–26   26 and over

ANNUAL PRECIPITATION (cm)

20–24   25–49   50–99   100–149   150 and over

Dwarfed by a mammoth sand dune, two horsemen cross a high valley of t

arid Xinjiang region in western China, near the borders with the Soviet Union and Afghanistan. Above the dune loom the jagged peaks of the Pamirs.

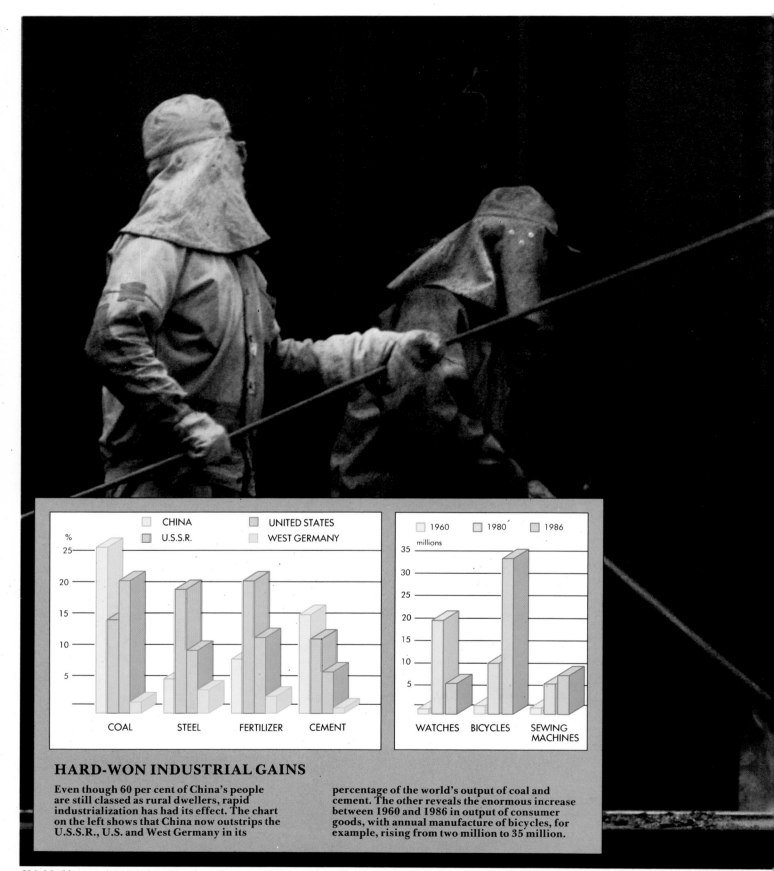

HARD-WON INDUSTRIAL GAINS

Even though 60 per cent of China's people are still classed as rural dwellers, rapid industrialization has had its effect. The chart on the left shows that China now outstrips the U.S.S.R., U.S. and West Germany in its percentage of the world's output of coal and cement. The other reveals the enormous increase between 1960 and 1986 in output of consumer goods, with annual manufacture of bicycles, for example, rising from two million to 35 million.

Shielded by special clothing that gives them protection against the intense heat, three workers at the Shijingshan plant near Peking tend a furnace

10

converting coal into coke, which is then used to make steel from iron ore.

Fishermen pole their slender scows on the River Li in south-eastern China. Lamps are hung over the water to serve as an attractant, and tame cormorant

GROWING MORE FOOD

Except during the famine years in the early 1960s, the overall food supply per person in China has been steadily increasing since the Communist takeover. Marine and freshwater fish are a major source of protein. The freshwater catch is greater than that of any other nation; while roughly half the freshwater catch is wild, the other half is bred in ponds or, increasingly, in flooded paddy fields.

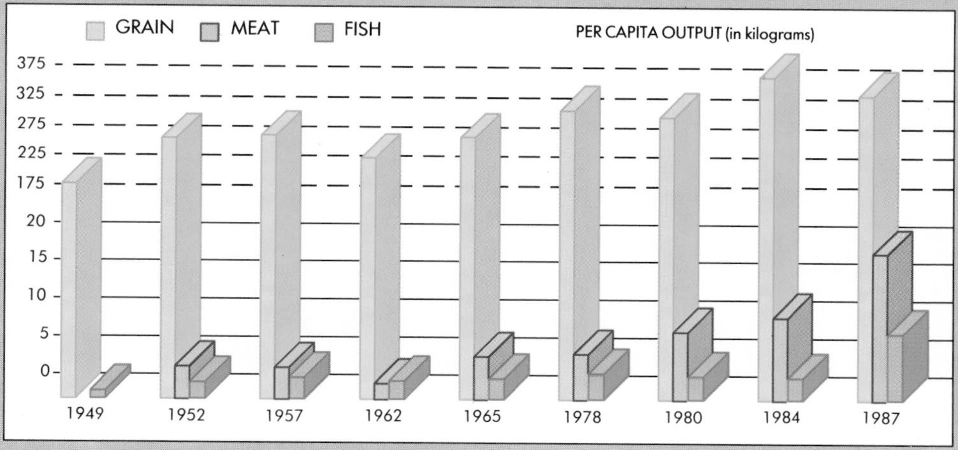

GRAIN MEAT FISH   PER CAPITA OUTPUT (in kilograms)

375
325
275
225
175
20
15
10
5
0

1949 1952 1957 1962 1965 1978 1980 1984 1987

are employed to dive and catch the fish. Collars round the birds' necks keep them from swallowing their prey, which is later pulled from their beaks.

13

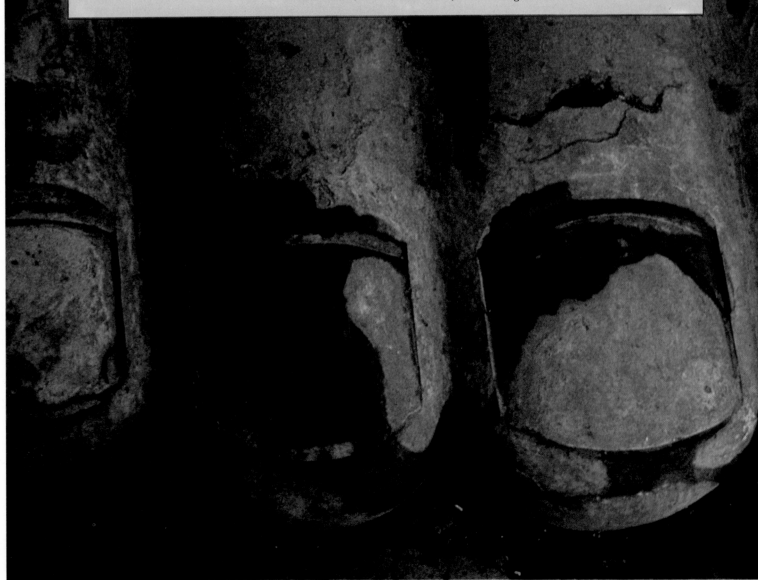

THE PERSISTENCE OF RELIGIOUS LIFE

Although China's present government is atheist, its constitution guarantees religious freedom. By and large the promise is kept. Three world religions—Buddhism, Islam, and Roman Catholic and Protestant Christianity—survive along with folk beliefs and the ancient philosophies of Confucianism and Daoism.

The earliest imported religion, Buddhism, came from India in the first century B.C. Before the 1949 Communist takeover, there were half a million Buddhist monks and nuns; 40,000 temples and monasteries dotted the land, along with uncounted statues of the Buddha—some monumental, as here. Since then, the number of clerics has shrunk, but the great yearly festivals go on.

Islam, introduced to China by Arab traders in the seventh century, thrives largely among the minority peoples of the north-west, although there are faithful even in Peking.

Christianity, which arrived from Europe in the 16th century, has been strictly controlled by government regulations. All foreign missionaries were expelled in the 1950s; churches were forced to become autonomous Chinese bodies, divorced from their brethren elsewhere. Even so, there has been a revival of Christian worship— a development viewed with alarm by the government.

A blue-clad Chinese worker meditates peacefully on the time-stained toe of a colossal statue of the Buddha in Sichuan province. The figure was erected

uring the Tang Dynasty (618–907), when the growing popularity of Buddhism coincided with great artistic activity.

China is a land of extremes in almost every respect—size, climate, population, industrial development, even history. The third largest nation on earth, it covers 9.56 million square kilometres, reaching from sub-Arctic wastes to the tropics. In its forbidding west, 3,200 kilometres inland from the sea, are deserts too dry and too hot or cold for extensive settlement. In the south-west rises the inhospitable Tibetan plateau, averaging 4,400 metres in altitude.

China is the oldest of great nations, its dynamic history stretching 4,000 years in an unbroken span. Some works of long-ago emperors have never been equalled. The Grand Canal—longest on the globe—was dug in the seventh century A.D. to connect the north with the rice-growing Yangtze valley, 1,800 kilometres to the south. It required 5.5 million labourers, kept on the job by 50,000 guards. Some 900 kilometres are still in use, carrying barges between Hangzhou and the Yellow River. The Chinese also built the largest structure ever erected, the Great Wall, completed 2,000 years ago. It writhes 6,000 kilometres through valleys and over mountains from the coast north-east of Peking to the deserts of Inner Mongolia.

But the most significant superlative applies to population: China is—and long has been—the most populous nation; in 1762 a census counted 200 million people, perhaps twice the number than in Western Europe. Today the count exceeds one billion. (India is second with 700 million.) A Chinese, wrote scholar John K. Fairbank, "is seldom in all his life beyond earshot of other people."

Until 1911 the government of these throngs consisted of a huge bureaucracy headed by an emperor. That year, the last imperial ruler was toppled by young reformers organized by an idealistic physician, Sun Yat-sen. The country soon fell into chaos, centralized government disintegrated, and various regions were controlled by contending factions: individual warlords; the Nationalist Party of Sun Yat-sen and his brother-in-law, Chiang Kai-shek; and a growing Communist organization. The man who emerged as leader of the Communists, Mao Tse-tung, perceived that success depended on winning over peasant farmers. He proclaimed that the peasants, properly led, would "rise like a mighty storm". In the 1930s and 1940s he harnessed this storm, partly through land reform, partly through propaganda, partly through iron discipline over his armies. His troops—unlike the usual run of rapacious soldiers known to the peasants—"were always courteous," one farmer recalled. "They did not enter your house unless invited, and they asked politely for food." Victory came in 1949.

Mao swiftly attempted to convert agrarian China into a powerful industrial nation. But with little home-grown capital and only parsimonious help from the Soviet Union, expansion required painful diversion of resources from agriculture and consumer goods to industry. But in the next four decades railway track increased from 22,000 kilometres to 54,000, the road network grew from 75,000 kilometres to nearly one million, and the gross national product rose from 83 billion Chinese dollars to 1,590 billion, according to official figures.

Much of the nation's manufacturing vigour is concentrated in big cities along the eastern coast. Shanghai and its suburbs, which have textile, steel and shipbuilding industries, are home to 11 million people, more than live in either New York or London. China's largest city, however, is Chongqing in Sichuan, with a population of some 14 million. Peking is home to nine million and is a centre of the iron and steel, petrochemical and automotive industries. It also contains the 40-hectare Tiananmen Square, 10 massive public buildings that were constructed in 10 months, and the Forbidden City, 100 hectares of palaces and gardens once reserved for the imperial family.

Peking is one of the world's most uncomfortable capitals, blazing hot in summer, freezing in winter and blanketed in spring by yellow dust blown in from the Gobi Desert. West of Peking lie other huge deserts, which the nation's leaders have urgently tried to develop. Each year throughout the 1960s and into the 1970s hundreds of thousands of young people from the overcrowded east were forcibly sent west to work in new mines or factories, to prospect for oil or metals, or to construct irrigation projects.

Social engineering on this scale is possible because the People's Republic is based on systematic and dictatorial control by the Chinese

Wearing ornate ceremonial robes, a monk belonging to a Lamaist Buddhist monastery walks towards a temple in Peking in 1913. This rare old colour picture, made by the obsolete Autochrome process, is one of 72,000 commissioned by French banker Albert Kahn, who dispatched photographers to record life in countries around the world.

Communist Party. After Mao's death in 1976, the rigid political system was retained, but there was an easing of the Party bonds constraining the economy, with integration in a single world economy accepted as a necessary goal. Following initial successes, this strategy ran into serious difficulties in the late 1980s, when rampant inflation and corruption discredited the government and led to serious social unrest. In June 1989, China's hardline leaders reacted to demands for a greater degree of democracy by ordering the massacre of young protestors occupying Tiananmen Square. The veterans of China's Communist Revolution had braved one more storm, but they had alienated an entire generation of youth—China's future. "China's reforms are not an issue that can be decided by the few," insisted a leading Chinese economist. "Rather they proceed according to the will of one billion people who want to eat and become rich."

Three classes make up the Chinese nation: peasant farmers like the man above, who are still 80 per cent of the population; industrial workers, who now include women such as the oil-field worker in the centre; and a bureaucracy represented by the customs official on the right.

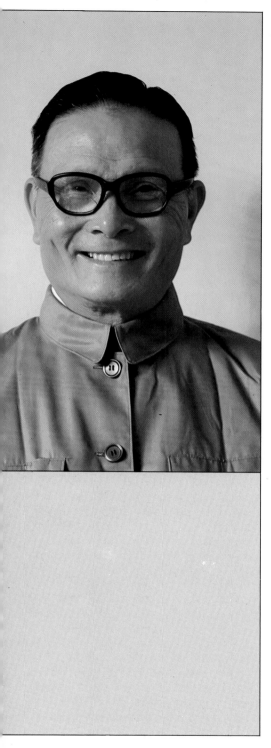

OLD WAYS AMID RADICAL CHANGE

In a climactic chapter of the 18th-century Chinese novel *Dream of the Red Chamber*, a father punishing his son is upbraided by the youth's grandmother. "Kill me first and then you can kill him!" she shouts. The father stops, as a man in any culture might be expected to do when confronted by objections from an elderly parent. But this is China. The power of the grandmother is awesome, and there follows a scene of submission so total as to be unimaginable in the West.

The father—an imperial official and a leader of one of the richest clans in the country—falls to the floor and beats his brow on the tiles, begging forgiveness. The grandmother wheels and marches off, accompanied by maids, the youthful miscreant and—bringing up the rear, uttering cries of apology—the chastened lord of the household.

This incident is fiction of times gone by. Nonetheless, the grandmotherly power that it illustrates was not only a reality in 18th-century China, but is also very much a reality today. Not long ago in a village in Shaanxi province, a nine-year-old girl rebelled against school and refused to attend. Her parents objected. She fled to her grandmother, who took the child in her arms and shooed away the parents.

The cadre—responsible official—of the community intervened. In modern China, the government insists on school for all children, even those of poor farmers. Truancy is not taken lightly. Still, the cadre's authority got him nowhere. The grandmother was obdurate. Neither the traditional authority of the parents nor the power of the Communist state could shake an old woman's control over her grandchild. The girl remained under the grandmother's protection for a year before deciding to go back to school.

Such continuity of past and present is by no means rare. Old China lives on in a thousand ways—in the way children are brought up, in obedience to authority, in frugal living, in reliance on patience and persuasion to get things done, in government by an enormous bureaucracy. (A university professor in the city of Tianjin estimates that one in seven people in that city is a Communist Party bureaucrat or a member of a bureaucrat's family.)

Bureaucracy and family remain dominant in China, as they have since at least the third century B.C. In the old days, the family formed the basic structure of Chinese society, each family controlling the behaviour of its members, providing them with work and seeing to their welfare. Today, families still have opportunities to look after their own in matters of employment. For example, upon retirement a factory worker can sometimes pass his job down to a son or daughter. And a rural peasant seeking a better life in the city depends on relatives living there to help him gain the necessary governmental permission to move. Within the

1

For all the constancy of Chinese culture—the world's oldest, with an unbroken tenure of more than 4,000 years—the country has seen profound and often violent changes. Its people have endured foreign interference and internal turmoil—revolutions, civil war, forced migrations, political upheavals. Some of the greatest changes have occurred in the last few decades. Power once exercised by semi-feudal landowners and private enterprises has been seized by the state, which now owns all the land and most industries, and attempts to regulate even intimate details of private lives.

In modern-day China, many foods and some personal possessions are rationed; urban housing is allotted; jobs are assigned (sometimes a husband and wife are sent to widely separated cities); travel requires permission, not easily obtained. In many places, young couples must seek state approval to have a baby.

A number of changes have been undeniably positive for the majority of the population. Since the Communists won control in 1949—an event known simply as Liberation—beggars have almost disappeared from city streets and bandit gangs have vanished from the countryside. A whole generation has grown up without the tragic experience of famine, and literacy has jumped from 15 per cent in 1949 to more than 75 per cent today.

To some degree the mix of old and new influences the lives of all Chinese, but the effects vary greatly in different parts of this huge country. China is big by any measure. Its 9.56 million square kilometres make it the third largest country in the world; only the Soviet Union and Canada are bigger. Sprawling from the Pacific to the Himalayas—

family, the elderly still hold their places of esteem; in a family meeting, counsel will be sought deferentially from even a senile grandfather, although his advice may not be heeded.

The powers of the family and the ruling bureaucracy are intricately intertwined. In the old days, the head of a clan was usually some kind of imperial official. Today, only the names are changed. Chinese farmers go along with the Communist organization of agriculture because it follows family lines. The party cadre who directs work is seldom a stranger dispatched from Peking but most often a prominent member of the local clan; the members of an economic cooperative, who labour

together in the fields, are almost always closely related—and when efficiency dictates that a team be enlarged by the addition of more-distant relatives, the change can be effected only after prolonged and difficult negotiations.

The continuing importance of influence and persuasion—as opposed to the imposition of codified rules—can be seen in the case of the girl who would not go to school. The cadre defied by the grandmother did not summon the old woman to court for violating a school attendance law, as his opposite number in the West might have done; technically no such law exists in China. He applied pressure, waited, and eventually achieved the desired result.

about 3,800 kilometres from east to west—China has an extraordinary array of environments: sub-tropical wetlands, river deltas, open prairie, rolling hills and high plateaux, bleak deserts and forbidding mountains. Most of the country is so dry, cold and barren that it is uninhabitable, or nearly so. Yet a small part of the land is very habitable indeed.

China is far and away the most populous nation on earth. It is home to a fifth of all human beings alive today: more than a billion people, over four times the population of the United States. Ninety per cent of the people live on only one sixth of the land, jammed into the marvellously fertile valleys of three major rivers, the Yellow in the north, the Yangtze in the south and the West still further south.

It is in the densely populated lower reaches of these river valleys, in the eastern part of the country, that the modern way of life can best be observed. Here are found cities and industrial suburbs and intensely cultivated agricultural land. Here live farm hands and street sweepers, ballet dancers and lathe operators, film makers and soldiers, politicians and space scientists. Most of these people can be grouped into three broad categories, each including many levels of power, prestige and economic compensation. One category consists of professionals and white-collar workers, whether surgeons, farm managers, teachers or officials in charge of ration coupons. Another is made up of workers in industry and commerce. Farmers represent a third category, and they far outnumber the others. Some 80 per cent of the Chinese labour force work the land (in France, only 8 per cent of the working population are farmers, and in the United States, just 3 per cent).

Among the farmers and craftsmen of rural areas, the old Chinese ways survive most noticeably. The government has tried several schemes of organizing agriculture into large and small units such as village and township enterprises and economic cooperatives. But Chinese farming still centres around the old market towns, and the work is still done in small fields by family groups. Moreover, farmers possess a measure of economic freedom. Whereas the members of the other two categories are all salaried state employees, farmers are allowed to earn some independent income by producing and selling crops of their own and engaging in small enterprises such as producing soft drinks or refining cooking oil.

Typical of the more prosperous farming families is one headed by a retired carpenter named Jiang, who lives in a rice-growing village 50 kilometres north of the southern port city of Canton. Because of its mild climate, the area produces two crops of rice a year and, during the winter months, a third crop of barley or winter wheat.

But the village does not live on rice alone; it also raises pigs. In fact, the farm unit of which it is a part contains more pigs than people—70,000. The founder of the modern Chinese state, Mao Tse-tung, once called the pig a walking fertilizer factory, and farmers exploit that virtue. One of Jiang's neighbours, Zhang Liyi, claims that his small flock of pigs produces about a tonne of fertilizer a year. Furthermore, Zhang says he can sell each of his pigs in the adjacent market town for more than twice the monthly salary earned by a son who works in a coal mine.

Because year-round farming is possible in this climate, work is continual. Jiang and his neighbours often bike or take a bus into Canton for a day of shopping or recreation.

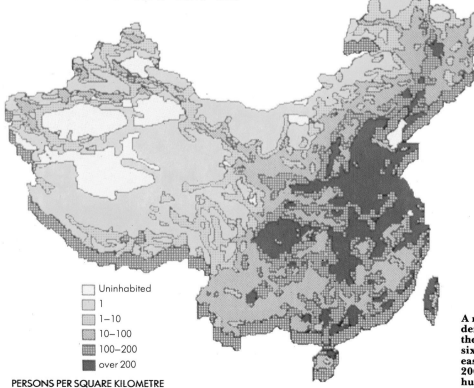

Uninhabited
1
1–10
10–100
100–200
over 200

PERSONS PER SQUARE KILOMETRE

A map colour-keyed to population density shows China's plight: most of the population is jammed into one sixth of the nation's land. The fertile east central region holds more than 200 persons per square kilometre; huge western areas are uninhabited.

Surrounded by mist-shrouded pinnacles of limestone, the city of Guilin is best known for its scenic setting, but it is also a commercial centre—a

hub of rail and river transport in South China.

Jiang lives in a stone-floored brick house in a complex of other dwellings. The house has been owned by his family for about a century; at any one time, members of several generations have lived under its roof. Like most village housing, the building—but not the land it stands on—is private property, and Jiang does not have to pay rent. A sleeping loft was added over one of the bedrooms to accommodate his sizeable family: his wife, a son and daughter-in-law, and seven grandchildren, the oldest of whom is actually away, serving in the army. The son is also a part-time resident; he works in a grain-husking mill several kilometres away and is home only on his day off.

Compared with the housing of many Chinese farm families, the Jiangs' home is quite luxurious. It has two stoves in a kitchen and, off to one side, a breezeway with tables and stools for outdoor dining in good weather. On the opposite side, the kitchen opens on to a courtyard with a well and a combined bathhouse-toilet, which drains into a gutter along the outside wall of the house. (Solid waste is collected for fertilizer, as it is everywhere in China.)

The home has two bedrooms divided by partitions, one to provide a living room, the other, a sewing room-storeroom. In the storeroom the Jiangs keep root vegetables and large earthenware jars of feed for their chickens and ducks. The living room opens on to the courtyard through a wide doorway that floods the room with light. It is furnished with two tables, four chairs and several stools. On the walls hang family photographs in handcrafted wooden frames, a mirror, a pendulum clock and a poster for the Peking Opera, which presents elaborately costumed, stylized dramatizations of traditional legends. The room also contains a bust of Mao and several plants.

Although Jiang is retired, he still rises early. "My day begins at 5 o'clock, when I get up and go to the teahouse to meet my friends and drink." By seven he is back at the house, helping his wife, the family matriarch, in a traditional task, "taking care of the youngest children while my daughter-in-law works in the rice fields." His wife, who was a field-worker until she retired, manages the household chores. She is keeper of the family finances, but, says Jiang, she is generous: "She does not refuse money when one asks."

Her generosity is supported by multiple incomes. Jiang's pension is 70 per cent of his previous salary, and he does odd carpentry jobs for his family and neighbours: "I spend some time each day building tables, chairs or doors, and repairing furniture." But as everywhere in China, the pace is usually unhurried. There are frequent breaks for gossip, and at midday Jiang takes two or three hours for lunch and a nap. "We eat dinner at six, and after dinner I read the newspaper or listen to the radio." By 8 o'clock he is in bed.

The Jiangs are able to save a good part of their cash income. The family's private plot supplies most of their vegetables, and the economic cooperative to which they belong provides them with grain, cereal and firewood.

"We spend much of our money on clothing," Jiang says, but the outlay per person would hardly buy a shirt in the West. The money mainly goes on materials, for most clothing is homemade and its cut is standardized. Men and boys wear shorts; women and girls, trousers; and toddlers wear the eminently practical split pants *(page 24)*, made up in bright, patterned colours.

23

1

The Jiangs of South China are considerably better off than the Lius of Liuling village in the north, a region Mao once described from first-hand knowledge as "poor, backward, underdeveloped and mountainous". Home for Zhenyong, Yangjing and their three young children is a cave, but such living quarters also have their advantages. The front of the cave is a large opening with a door and wooden-framed windows covered by translucent oil paper to admit light. Inside, there are rooms that are cool in summer and easy to keep warm in winter with a *kang*, or stove-bed, a clay platform with a fire underneath.

The Liu home is one of many carved in rows up a hillside to form a kind of vertical village. Even the community's administrative centre is housed in a cave. Such earthen cave dwellings, long used in this region of steep but easily excavated hills, free the available flat land on the hilltop and the valley floor for crops. And a cave house is easy to build: in 40 working days, a team of four or five can construct one that will last 30 years without the need for any major repairs.

Both adult Lius work in the fields alongside their relatives. The labour is arduous. They have oxen to pull wooden ploughs, but no machinery. Only about half the farmland in China is ploughed with tractors.

The main crop is winter wheat; local farmers, like those everywhere in China, must fill a quota; once the quota has been filled, each family then sells any surplus. Also grown are potatoes, cabbages (often turned into sauerkraut), beans, tomatoes, melons, onions, corn and millet; some produce is sold, but most of it is used for food.

Millet, a type of cereal, provides the

grain that is the basis of these farmers' diet. Almost every meal consists of a bowl of "golden rice", or millet porridge, served with stir-fried vegetables. Instead of tea, the Lius often drink a thin millet gruel, and in winter Yangjing makes a fermented millet wine. Even the village dogs eat millet and vegetables; except at hog-slaughtering time, they are vegetarian dogs.

For much of the growing season the Lius' working day begins at 5 a.m. Zhenyong goes straight to the fields, without breakfast. At about eight, one of the workers makes the rounds of the households, picking up bowls of food for those in the fields. "We take turns," explains a team leader. "The one who is doing it of course begins to work later. He gets work credit for fetching our

A girl feeds a toddler dressed in split pants, the typical garb of young children. In contrast to their elders, who wear sombre clothes, most of the youngsters wear bright colours.

food. It isn't easy carrying dishes with food for 10 people."

After Yangjing joins the field-workers, an elderly sister-in-law looks after the children (this would normally be a grandmother's role, but the Lius' grandparents are dead). Depending on the season, Yangjing may weed, turn patches of earth the ox-drawn plough cannot reach, or help with the harvesting and threshing. At noon, she goes home to make the midday meal. For Zhenyong there is then an hour's nap, but Yangjing sometimes goes to the river with the family washing.

By three, husband and wife are back in the fields again, where they remain until 7 or 8 p.m. "When I come home in the evening," says Yangjing, "the first thing is to feed the family; then feed the pig and the hen and her six chicks. Then I see to the children and, when they are asleep, I do my sewing and make clothes and such until 10 o'clock, when I am tired and fall asleep."

In summer, the busiest season, Zhenyong and Yangjing rise at four and work until dark; "I do not sit up at night sewing," says Yangjing. In winter, they do not rise until six, and Zhenyong has breakfast at home. It is during this time of little field work that most of the family's clothing is made.

For each member of the family Yangjing sews two jacket-and-trouser outfits, one quilted, the other unquilted. Often she must pick out the tiny stitches of a bedraggled quilted garment to salvage the batting within. Even the shell of such worn-out garments is put to use: although plastic sandals are popular, Yangjing frequently uses the fabric scraps, glued together in layers, to create soles for shoes—whose soles and uppers are sewn with thread she makes from jute.

Cave dwellings dot the steep terrain of a hillside in north central China. Using hand tools, a family can carve a warm, dry and even airy home, 3 by 5.5 metres, in just a few months.

1

Many of these domestic tasks are shared by her husband. In Liuling, it is customary for the men to do the knitting, and Zhenyong knits four pairs of stockings a year. He supplies the household with water, daily bringing up four bucketfuls from a nearby well. He also gathers firewood, and occasionally helps with the cleaning chores. Zhenyong does more than is usual for men in rural areas, and Yangjing's neighbours envy her. "Most men here," they say, "go straight to the *kang* and sleep when they get home from work." But Yangjing considers Zhenyong's assistance a mixed blessing: "He isn't as particular about housework as a woman is."

Although the city of Yan'an is within bicycling distance, the Lius do not get into town often—"once a month roughly," says Yangjing, "and then to shop and see the opera. If a good, famous opera company comes, I'll go in more often. But we never go together. That's because of the children. We can never go out together in the evenings."

The customs of country people like the Lius and Jiangs are lightly touched by the strictures of the state. Although the Communist government frowns upon elaborate observances of weddings and traditional holidays, which deplete the farmers' savings, such occasions as the Chinese New Year, the Grave-Sweeping Festival and the Mid-Autumn Moon Festival continue to be justification for feasts and celebration. And in many villages, marriages are still arranged by intermediaries—but both parties have the right to object if they are not satisfied with the choice of a mate. The ancient custom of the bride price is also still observed. Like a dowry in reverse, the bride price is supposed to compensate a father for the loss of his

daughter. The practice is forbidden, and when couples go to a registry office for a marriage certificate, they are expressly asked if money has changed hands. Most of them lie and say no.

In the cities far more than in the country, the everyday lives of people have been fundamentally reorganized since Liberation. The population of the urban centres includes not only the professionals and civil servants who have always played a major role in China, but also a growing army of industrial workers. Industry still absorbs only 10 to 14 per cent of the work force, but the numbers are large: more than

two million steelworkers, about six million transport workers, eight million construction workers.

A factory job is prized because it is secure. Despite sporadic attempts to increase worker productivity with bonuses and promotions linked to achievement, most people consider industry an "iron rice bowl". In the factory, men and women enjoy higher earnings than their country cousins. Once a job is gained, it is almost never lost, and a reasonably diligent worker can expect regular promotions. Most workers live near the job, often in a factory compound that may also provide such ser-

vices as a clinic, subsidized cafeteria, day nursery and school.

As in the countryside, the day begins at cockcrow for many workers. Shortly after 5 o'clock, dishevelled and sleepy-eyed, they converge on the communal washrooms in their blocks of flats, carrying pans, soap, toothbrushes and towels. After a noisy round of splashing, spitting and gargling, they spill out on to the streets for their morning exercise—*taijiquan* (shadow-boxing), jogging or the mock-martial movements of *wushu*. Breakfast is a simple meal: green tea, steamed buns or a bowl of rice gruel taken at home, in back-street restaurants on the way to work or in the factory cafeteria.

Rush hour is a clamorous tide of crammed articulated buses, traffic-dodging pedestrians and bicycles by the million. Factory workers put in an eight-hour day, but they take frequent breaks for tea and cigarettes. Lunch in the cafeteria consists of a bowl of vegetables, rice and perhaps a bit of meat. Afterwards, workers unroll their bedrolls on any flat surface—a desk, the floor or the top of a covered cart—and have a nap before returning to the job. And so it goes on, six days a week. Because days off are alternated, the factory never shuts down.

One city family has been described by Orville Schell, a writer who lived in China and worked on a commune and in a factory. In Shanghai, he visited the flat of Master Chen ("Master" denotes neither rank nor authority, but is a title of deference given to veteran workers). Chen worked in Workshop 11 of the Shanghai Electrical Machinery Factory, and his wife had a job in a factory store. They lived at Min Hang, a complex of five-storey buildings beyond the factory gates that contained depart-

ment stores, swimming pools, four middle schools, 15 primary schools and 80,000 residents.

The Chens shared a kitchen with three other families on the same floor. In the bedroom were trunks, a wardrobe and two double beds separated by a curtain—one bed for the three children, one for the parents. A wooden table, piled with polished apples, sweets, chewing gum and glasses of tea, occupied the centre of the room.

"There is such a difference between the life of us workers before Liberation and now," Chen proudly told Schell. "Before Liberation we only had small shacks and huts. And now look: we have flats. We only pay four yuan a month in rent [a yuan will buy about two kilograms of rice]. I make 90 yuan a month, and my wife 70 yuan. We even save a little money each month.

"In the evenings, I usually come home straight after work," he said, "and read or listen to the radio." He gestured to a red plastic radio. "I made it myself. Its tone is still not good. I must fix the bass. But I'm working on it." Chen turned to the open window, listening for a moment to the voices of children outside. "They are welcoming you," he said to his visitor.

Since the economy was liberalized in the 1970s, consumer goods have become much more widely available, though they are still expensive and distribution is uneven. In a department store, a worker may have to pay the equivalent of one to two months' earnings to buy an electric fan; three months' earnings (plus a certificate from work to confirm that it is a necessity) to buy a bicycle; and six to eight months' earnings to buy a small refrigerator or television set. A small household, comprising parents and

one child, probably has one bicycle (a car—unlike a colour TV—remains an impossible dream). There will almost certainly be a radio, a sewing machine and a wrist watch per adult.

This much comfort suffices for most Chinese, many of whom deliberately limit their ambitions to a place on the factory floor. They acknowledge two practical reasons. Such a job is essentially insulated from politics, and its holder cannot easily be caught in the crosscurrents of doctrine that have often swept managers and even minor officials from soft berths in the metropolitan centres to menial posts in the western desert. The second reason is simple economics. Advancement to a position of responsibility and authority does not bring a great change in the standard of living. It is true that a few of the most important people in the party, government and military enjoy appropriate luxury; spacious homes in walled gardens, chauffeured limousines, servants. But they are the exceptions. The gap between rich and poor, once so wide in China, is now much narrowed: in fact, the majority of people who work with their heads, commonly called the "intellectuals", are now materially worse off than manual workers.

Included in this group is the enormous army of bureaucrats that has always managed the details of Chinese life. In the days of the Empire, administrators and magistrates assigned from Peking governed every locality in the country. These early bureaucrats were selected by written examinations that tested their understanding of Confucian doctrine and their skill in composition and calligraphy. Aristocratic birth was not a necessity (although the rich, with easy

An elderly man in Peking performs his morning routine of *taijiquan* exercises. Practised daily by millions of Chinese, *taijiquan* evolved from a 17th-century martial art.

access to education, had an advantage), and poor youths sometimes rose to high position. Today, of course, the requirements are different. Marxist doctrine and competence are what count. And in an odd twist, humble ancestry is now desirable: advancement goes to those with "proper class background", that is, descent from a family of landless peasants.

Members of this new bureaucracy fit into a multi-tiered structure of rank that includes more than 20 different grades. Status is easily discerned by other Chinese in details of personal belongings—cushioning on an office chair, fabric and cut of clothes, even the number of jacket pockets, pens and jumpers worn. A Western journalist once irreverently described a high official as "a four-pocketed, three-ballpointed, six-layered, Shanghai-tailored responsible" person.

The major advantage of position in China is that it confers the power to trade favours in a covert system of influence peddling called the back door. Through the back door, the privileged gain the amenities of life.

In old China, bribery was ubiquitous. A common saying cautioned, "The gate to the magistrate's court is always open, but those without money should not enter." Venality of that sort was virtually eliminated in the early years of the People's Republic, but official corruption re-emerged during the chaos of the Cultural Revolution, and reached epidemic proportions in the 1980s, provoking widespread anger and disillusionment among the general population.

Some of the advantages of position can be glimpsed in the lifestyle of a certain Professor Zhao, vice chair of his department in a university. (The name is a pseudonym to protect him against possible criticism; at this level of Chinese society, private lives are not revealed freely. Zhao earns no more than a factory worker; many of his junior colleagues earn less. His wife, Yuling, is a schoolteacher on a salary that would be considered derisory by most manual workers. But rank has its privileges. Two sons, Weida and Xilian, are students at their father's university, their careers aided in minor ways by his position; for example, his "back door" gives them access to otherwise unobtainable books in the university library.

The Zhaos occupy an upstairs flat in a house that was built before Liberation. Four families, totalling 12 people, live in the five-room house, but the Zhaos rate two rooms, because they are the largest family and because of their superior rank. One room doubles as dining room and parents' bedroom; the other serves as both living room and bedroom for the boys.

On the Zhaos' floor is a bathroom, shared by all the tenants. It contains a bath and a toilet, but only the latter is used; there is no hot water, and all four families bathe at the bathhouses on the university campus. The Zhaos have partitioned off part of the bathroom to create a small private kitchen, in which they have installed a two-burner propane stove. The flat is heated by a wood stove, which is dangerous and dirty but more dependable than the central heating system. In most modern blocks of flats, boilers never seem adequate to the job.

The Zhaos are fortunate in their possessions. They own two television sets, one a colour TV; a stereo system; an electric refrigerator and a washing machine. Their furnishings include an upholstered couch, two desks, several chairs, a folding card table on which they eat, and three beds. The parents' bed has springs, the sons' have cushioned wooden platforms. The family also owns a sewing machine, several small electronic calculators, four bicycles and four wrist watches. Some of these possessions were purchased by Zhao on trips abroad.

Besides the parents' salaries, the family members receive monthly allotments of coupons for rice, cooking oil and wheat flour. Professor Zhao and his wife used to shop for groceries every day; now that they have a refrigerator, they usually shop every other day. Meat is expensive, and so they only buy one half or one quarter jin (a jin is about half a kilogram) for the four of them. They like pork best. Fish is costly and hard to get, and shellfish is scarcer still. Weida says he has eaten prawns "only once in my 20 years". Vegetables, when in season, are inexpensive, and cucumbers, *baicai* (Chinese cabbage) and string beans are favourites.

Domestic duties other than shopping are shared. Zhao often prepares breakfast; his wife and sons have to be at school by 7.30, but he can do research and writing at home most mornings. Yuling does most of the cooking, however—including a family lunch at home—and the boys are responsible for cleaning up.

The Zhaos spend most evenings at home, watching television or reading. They usually watch the news—which often includes excerpts from Western news broadcasts—English language lessons, variety shows and dubbed Western adventure series. Although the Zhaos like films and opera and could afford to go, none of them can

Jogging is a relatively new addition to the many varieties of exercise that Chinese do anywhere outdoors—in parks, on streets, even at bus stops.

1

spare two hours in a ticket queue that fills up at five in the morning for an evening performance. Of course, if the Zhaos had a larger "back door", they could get tickets without queuing.

In Peking, American journalist Richard Bernstein made friends with a more typical young couple whom he referred to as Wang and Li. Both were employed in clerical jobs at the middle level of government. They owned a TV, a Japanese refrigerator and a large old-fashioned radio with a new stereo cassette player attached. Yet they and their four-year-old son lived in a single room in a dormitory. And when Bernstein asked them how they spent an average day, the answer he got revealed much about the frustrations of life in modern China.

"Wang and Li," wrote Bernstein, "wake up on the average morning at 7 o'clock. They get their son ready for the office day nursery. In their dormitory, there is 15 minutes of hot water every morning for those who want to bathe; this is done in dim, grimy common bathrooms, one for men and one for women. They rush through this activity not only because of the shortness of time but also because breakfast food goes on sale in the dormitory canteen just when the hot water arrives in the bathrooms. So by this piece of illogical planning, it often happens that they can have a bath but not breakfast or breakfast but not a bath, since the food sells out very quickly.

"They both work from about 8 to 11.30 in the morning and from 1.30 to 5 in the afternoon. Wang goes to his job by bicycle (20 minutes) and Li to hers by bus (40 minutes). They try to divide most of the household chores, with wife Li in charge of the child, house cleaning and cooking, and husband Wang

A HANDY GUIDE TO EVERYDAY WORDS

train	火车	huoche	China	中国	Zhongguo
station	火车站	huochezhan	how much?	多少	duoshao
bus	公共汽车	gonggong qiche	I don't understand	我不懂	wo budong
bus stop	车站	chezhan	yes	是	shi
taxi	出租汽车	chuzu qiche	no	不是	bushi
aeroplane	飞机	feiji	please	请	qing
airport	飞机场	feijichang	thank you	谢谢	xiexie
hotel	旅馆	lüguan	sorry	对不起	duibuqi
restaurant	饭馆	fanguan	welcome	欢迎	huanying
tea	茶	cha	hello, how are you	你好	nihao
hot water	开水	kaishui	good-bye	再见	zaijian
hospital	医院	yiyuan	yesterday	昨天	zuotian
market	市场	shichang	today	今天	jintian
park	公园	gongyuan	tomorrow	明天	mingtian
museum	博物馆	bowuguan	open	开门	kaimen
factory	工厂	gongchang	closed	关门	guanmen
store	商店	shangdian	entrance	入口	rukou
toilet	厕所	cesuo	exit	出口	chukou
tourist	旅客	lüke	left	左	zuo
female	女	nü	right	右	you
male	男	nan	danger	危险	weixian
one	一	yi	be careful	小心	xiaoxin
two	二	er	front	前	qian
three	三	san	back	后	hou
four	四	si			
five	五	wu			
six	六	liu			
seven	七	qi			
eight	八	ba			
nine	九	jiu			
ten	十	shi			

Common Chinese words and phrases are listed with their translations. Next to them are transliterations in *pinyin (opposite page)*, China's official system for substituting Western letters for sounds.

taking responsibility for the laundry and the shopping. It is the latter that infuriates him. He says that he often tries to sneak away from work at around 11 in the morning to make some purchases, which can take him as much as an hour.

"Except for a bimonthly purchase of rice and wheat flour, he scarcely bothers with the state market because that is always too crowded and badly supplied. So, he takes his chances at the free market, paying the somewhat higher prices in exchange for the shorter waits. His rule of thumb is that if there are more than 20 people ahead of him in a line, he does not stand in it."

For Wang and Li, the ultimate frustration had occurred when they had tried to buy lamb to entertain their American friend at a meal in their home, but had failed and so had to accept his offer of dinner in his hotel instead. "Wang, fuming over his loss of face, hurled down a challenge. 'You foreigners live in this hotel where everything is provided. You never have to cram into a bus in the middle of a hot August day to get somewhere or have to ride your bicycle against the wind in January. So, you're completely out of touch with the way we old hundred surnames live,'" he said, using the Chinese term for average folk. He continued, "'But, try this: make believe that you are going to prepare a dinner for four people. Draw up a list of all the things you need. The meat, the vegetables, the oil, the cornflour, the soy sauce, et cetera. Then go out and try to buy it all. See if you succeed, see how long it takes before you finally realize that you are going to fail.'"

In the daily routines of such people as the Wangs, the Zhaos, the Lius and the Jiangs can be seen how much and

PRONOUNCING CHINESE

Sounds of *pinyin* transliterations are below, with equivalents in the older Wade-Giles system. Except for well-known names such as Peking, this book uses *pinyin*, which was adopted by the Chinese government in 1979.

PINYIN	ENGLISH EQUIVALENT	WADE-GILES
a	as in far	a
b	as in be	p
c	as in its	ts'
ch	as in chip	ch'
d	as in do	t
e	as in her	e
f	as in foot	f
g	as in go	k
h	as in her	h
i	as in eat, or as in sir	i
j	as in jeep	ch
k	as in kind	k'
l	as in land	l
m	as in mock	m
n	as in no	n
o	as in law	o
p	as in par	p'
q	as in cheek	ch'
r	as in right	j
s	as in sister	s, ss, sz
sh	as in shore	sh
t	as in top	t'
u	as in too	u, ü
w	as in want	w
x	as in she	hs
y	as in yet	y
z	as in zero	ts, tz
zh	as in jump	ch

how little China has changed. Traditional values persist within close regimentation. Life is generally better, though spartan, for nearly everyone. The majority of the Chinese people still farm village fields by the sweat of their brows. Yet by the mid-1980s China ranked fourth among the world's major steel producers, and seventh among oil producers.

An estimated 270,000 scientists, engineers and computer analysts are doing research on such things as nuclear weapons and space vehicles. The arts, carefully watched, are beginning to flourish after decades of disruption: by the early 1980s, seven professional music schools were open, there were 2,000 acting companies, and 3,000 literary journals had reappeared. China's army of some three million men and women is the largest armed force in the world.

Beyond the three river valleys that are home to nearly all of the Chinese lie two thirds of the nation, sparsely peopled by "officially recognized minorities", who are citizens of China but not considered Chinese. Although they make up only 6 per cent of the entire population, they total more human beings than live in France—and their lives generally differ from those of the Chinese more than Chinese ways differ from French ways.

Even within the limited area occupied by the multitude of people who do consider themselves Chinese, there is great diversity. The inhabitants of the south look different from those of the north, behave differently, and speak dialects so different that they are mutually unintelligible. This, then, is the marvel of China: that manyness and oneness are both evident to such a remarkable degree.

TASKS OF A FARM FAMILY

Photographs by Richard D. Gordon

The Chinese countryside, despite many changes wrought under Communist rule, seems a fabled place where time has stood still—not just for a few decades but for centuries. The farm family shown here and on the following pages lives in a prosperous village and is free of the desperate poverty and ever-present threat of starvation that were the rule in the old days. But the lifestyle of this family—the Guos—differs little from that of their ancestors. Three generations continue to live together in the same two-room dwelling. Everyone, including the family matriarch *(centre, below and right)*, works at tasks virtually unchanged for millennia.

The North China village in which the Guos reside has several small industries, but farming is the people's main occupation. The village is in high plateau country where winters are cold, so the main crop is a hardy strain of corn. For the Guos and other villagers it supplies a golden harvest around which all else revolves.

In a three-generation portrait of the Guos, Zhiming, the father, Xian, the mother, and their three older sons flank grandmother Guo and the youngest boy, Haifang. Behind them is the farmhouse door, ringed with good-luck symbols and, on the wall, a tiny Buddhist altar.

In a break from chores, Xian keeps busy by braiding rope from jute fibres while grandmother Guo enjoys a cigarette. This is the family's main room, decorated with photographs and prints and used for relaxing, dining and sleeping. A bed and the house's heating stove are on the right.

A TIMELESS ROUND OF CHORES

Three villagers pitch kernels of corn into the air with wooden shovels so that the husks will blow away, while Xian uses a home-made broom to tidy the pile. In the background is a state-owned sawblade factory.

Leiching, the Guo family's eldest son, heads for the fields on his horse-drawn cart, with a basket to collect manure, the main fertilizer in China. As a full-time carter, Leiching earns more work points per day, 15, than the 12 his father receives as a field hand.

As a horse nuzzles his back, Zhiming pauses for a cigarette break in the old communal village stable. He keeps his own mule in a shed near his house.

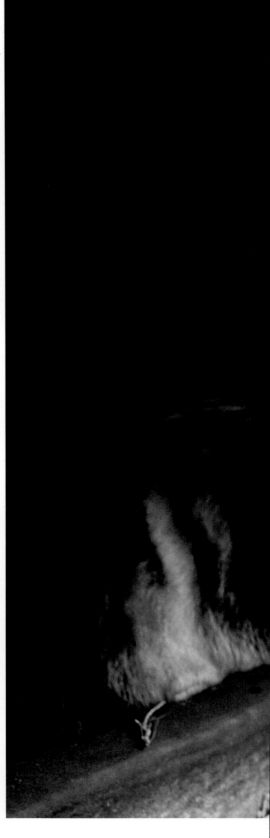

First-year pupils, including Haifang *(second row, second from right)*, **wear coats and hats in class because the school makes careful use of its coal supply.**

A teacher gives a pupil some extra maths lessons in the village school. The spartan furniture includes a portable stove, used only in winter, with a flue that sticks through a window. Most Chinese children today are educated at least until they are 14.

Leiching looks on as his younger brother Sanching struggles with his homework on a stone table in a courtyard of the farmhouse, where chickens roam next to the brick pigsty *(background)*. The tree is wrapped to protect it from bark-munching.

37

IN CHARGE AT HOME: GRANDMOTHER

Working patiently, Grandmother Guo discards the chaff from millet that she retrieved after the earlier winnowing process. Close by her stunted feet—bound during childhood before the practice was eradicated—the family's pig rests, while a rabbit scrounges lunch nearby.

Snapping pods with the assistance of her grandson Haifang and two other children, grandmother Guo shells peas for the evening meal. The farmhouse courtyard is the focus of most work and other family activities on mild and sunny days.

Bargaining with a pedlar, grandmother Guo watches him weigh her corn on a portable scale. She barters the kernels for a measure of *doufu*, the bean-curd product that provides much of the protein in the Chinese diet. The *doufu* man cycles through the village twice a week, tapping his handlebars with a mallet (*background*) to advertise his wares.

In preparation for lunch, Xian sifts cornmeal into a much-used cabinet drawer. On the left is the family's coal-fed cooking stove.

FILLING MEALS FROM A STEAMY KITCHEN

Xian pushes down on the handle of a press, fabricated by the village metal workers, that squeezes dough into long, rich yellow noodles. A wok steams with vegetables that will be added to pork to form the rest of the meal.

Grandmother Guo deftly turns the cooking meat—pork with the fat still attached. Farm families, whose diets include little oil, both need and enjoy fat as part of their food.

Before lunch, Zhiming helps his youngest son, Haifang, wash his hands in a bowl just outside the farmhouse door.

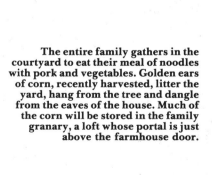

The entire family gathers in the courtyard to eat their meal of noodles with pork and vegetables. Golden ears of corn, recently harvested, litter the yard, hang from the tree and dangle from the eaves of the house. Much of the corn will be stored in the family granary, a loft whose portal is just above the farmhouse door.

Water buffaloes level and till a flooded field in order to prepare a paddy near the craggy Stone Forest of Yunnan province in the south-east, China's rice-growing region. The stone pillars, limestone pushed up by the shifting earth, were carved by rain and wind.

THE FOUR WORLDS OF A VARIED LAND

Spring breezes move the hundred grasses,
Fragrant orchids grow along my hedge.

That is one China, a garden-like meadow so lush and rich that a rice farmer can coax two and sometimes three crops from his plot of waterlogged ground in a single year.

The fields are chill; the sparse rain has stopped;
The colours of spring teem on every side.

That is another China, a broad treeless plain where stalks of wheat sway in the wind and a great river, alternately benevolent and viciously destructive, rolls to the sea between earthen dikes that are barn high.

Where the sky is like the sides of a tent
Stretched down over the Great Steppe
The sky is grey, grey:
And the steppe wide, wide.

This is a third China, a forsaken hard-pan desert, grey and wasted, raked by a pitiless wind.

A hundred leagues are sealed with ice,
A thousand leagues of whirling snow.

Still a fourth China is a sweep of ice-capped mountains broken by high valleys where herders peer from fur-fringed hoods and warm their callused hands over a feeble fire.

Each of these four starkly different terrains is characteristic of a wedge-shaped segment of a country that ranks first in the world in population, third in size. Its 9.56 million square kilometres spread west from the sea across Asia. India and Nepal share its south-western border; the Soviet Union lies to the north and Korea to the north-east; its southern frontier adjoins Burma, Laos and Vietnam.

Within this vastness are contrasts of every kind. China is the most agrarian nation on earth, yet only 11 per cent of its total area is good farmland—primarily in the three great basins of the Yellow, Yangtze and West Rivers. The rest is too steep, too cold or too dry. In the rainy sub-tropical south-east, summer holds perpetual sway; in the rainless wastes of the north-west, blazing summers alternate with bitter winters. The loftiest peaks, in the remote south-west, are higher than any in the Western hemisphere. Yet there is one depression in the north-west desert, containing an anomalous oasis named Turpan, that plunges 155 metres below sea level (the lowest place on earth, Sodom, on the Dead Sea, is 394 metres below sea level).

Cascading rivers fall through precipitous gorges in the south central highlands, to give China the potential for more hydroelectric power than any other country. Yet in the north delta flats, the Yellow River drops no more than 15 centimetres per kilometre in its final 800-kilometre run to the sea.

2

And though the country's coastline stretches from North Korea to Vietnam 5,600 kilometres along the Yellow Sea and the East and South China Seas, the far reaches of north-western Xinjiang are further from the ocean than anywhere else on the planet.

The landscape and the climate are not the only contrasts among the four major quadrants—south-east, north-east, north-west, south-west. The agriculture is necessarily different. So, naturally enough, are the foodstuffs. Even the people are different.

China, like most countries, is a mix of many dozens of ethnic groups. Living within the borders of the country and counted as its citizens—but not counted as Chinese people—are 55 officially designated minorities, all following customs and lifestyles of their own. They represent only a small fraction of the total population, but they number about 60 million. They have limited political autonomy; most of them live in the remote western provinces, far from the political and economic centre. But not all. One group, the rice-growing Zhuang, live right in the heart of China's most populous region, the south-eastern sun belt.

The Zhuang are surrounded on every side by the great majority of the population, the people who are considered Chinese. They call themselves Han, because all of them trace their ancestry to the founders of the Han Dynasty, a northern group who ruled China for approximately 400 years, beginning in 206 B.C. For two millennia, repeated invasions from the north brought in new conquerors to mix with the Han, simultaneously driving others south in successive waves to intermingle with peoples already living in those regions. Today the ethnic mix of the Han is much more diverse, encompassing myriad subgroups.

This steady flow of people towards the southern borders has made the Han united in culture but dissimilar in ethnic composition from region to region. The natives of Canton in the far south, for example, look different from those of Tianjin in the north; most southerners are slighter of build than

Han Chinese girl in traditional costume

northerners. And more important, they talk differently.

Though all Han Chinese employ the same written language *(Chapter 3)*, and technically they all speak the same language, they speak it in hundreds of dialects. In Canton, for example, they communicate in Cantonese; in Shanghai they speak Wu; in Fujian, the dialect is Min; and in Peking, it is Mandarin. Mandarin, the northern dialect of the imperial court, is the official Chinese of the government bureaucracy, but even educated southerners seldom use it among themselves.

Many of these dialects are mutually unintelligible. The character meaning "forest", for example, is pronounced "lin" in Mandarin, "lum" in Cantonese and "ling" in Min. Compounding the problem are musical variations in tone that give different meanings to the same word. Cantonese has eight separate tones, Mandarin has only four. Because of this phonetic confusion, a Cantonese farmer who speaks only his own dialect may not be able to communicate with a Wu-speaking Shanghai merchant or a Peking bureaucrat talking in Mandarin. Even Chinese films made in Hong Kong or Taiwan by Mandarin-speaking actors must be subtitled for Cantonese audiences.

The government is trying to unsnarl this linguistic tangle by encouraging all its people to speak Peking Mandarin, which in China is called *putonghua*. It is taught in the schools, now attended by virtually all children.

The common tongue of *putonghua* may help to lessen the ethnic and regional biases long notable in China. In 400 B.C. natives of the northern province of Shanxi were described (by southerners) as profit-loving; in the 20th century, as German sociologist Wolfram Eberhard discovered, these people were still considered business-minded. Similarly, northerners have often been less than admiring of southerners. Until recently, for example, the men of Fujian were derided as "three blades", capable only of using sharp instruments as tailors, barbers and cooks—work held in low esteem.

Author Lin Yutang described northerners as "hard living, tall and stalwart, hale, hearty, and humorous", and southerners as "inured to ease and culture and sophistication, mentally developed but physically retrograde, loving their poetry and their comforts, shrewd in business, gifted in *belles-lettres*, and cowardly in war".

Indeed, ease and culture might be expected in the south-east, for it is the richest of China's four quadrants. It contains the commercial centres of the great port cities of Shanghai and Canton, and the most productive farmland—the fertile basins of the Yangtze and West Rivers. It includes the alluvial coastal plains along the South and East China Seas and extends inland to the hills of Yunnan and Sichuan.

Here is the landscape that comes to the Westerner's mind when thinking of China. Warm and moist, green and usually frost-free, it is a gentle scene of soft-hued paddy fields and farmers in broad-brimmed hats tilling terraced hillsides. Near the city of Guilin, the

limestone bedrock that underlies hills has produced strange landscapes. Wind and water have sculpted this bedrock into weird-shaped pinnacles that rise directly from the ground, like giant bamboo shoots *(page 50)*, and have hollowed it into a maze of underground caves filled with stalactites and stalagmites. Its other-worldly beauty has inspired generations of artists.

Many of the forests that once covered this area were long ago cleared; only in Sichuan do bamboo wilds remain, as a preserve for the few surviving pandas. Swamps have been drained, and 2,000-year-old canals siphon off the excess water of monsoon-driven summer storms, simultaneously providing a network of waterways for transport. An annual rainfall averaging more than 150 centimetres, nearly three times

that of London, combines with subtropical warmth to give a year-round growing season. Even in the Sichuan uplands, winters are mild. An almost constant blanket of clouds protects the basin fields from the cooler air of the mountaintops. So seldom does the sun break through that Sichuan dogs, it is said, "bark when the sun shines".

The region's most spectacular feature is undoubtedly the great Yangtze River, which winds its sinuous way for 6,418 kilometres from the great mountains of Tibet to the sea, in the process draining an astonishing 1,958,000 square kilometres. Third-longest river in the world, exceeded only by the Nile and the Amazon, the Yangtze has several names, given to it at various times by the various peoples who have lived along it—Great River, Long River, River of Golden Sands. Marco Polo reported a journey on the Yangtze that "took upwards of 100 days", and he found that the river in some places was 16 kilometres from bank to bank.

Unlike the rampaging Yellow River, whose floods have caused enormous devastation, the Yangtze overflows its banks only about once a decade and seldom with great loss of life. And it is navigable to ocean-going ships far upstream, permitting such inland cities as Wuhan, which is some 700 kilometres from its mouth, to become major centres for industry.

Midway along its passage, as it passes through the Wushan Mountains, the river rushes through a series of gorges between sheer cliffs—"like a thousand seas," wrote the poet Su Dongpo, "poured into one cup". Once the bane of sailors whose frail craft splintered on rocks and shoals, the gorges of the Yangtze have been cleared of their worst obstacles and are

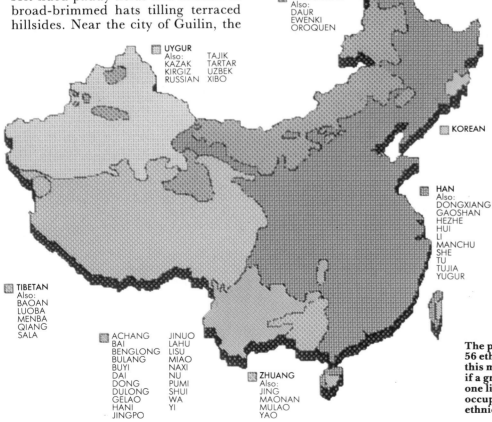

MONGOLIAN
Also:
DAUR
EWENKI
OROQUEN

UYGUR
Also: TAJIK
KAZAK   TARTAR
KIRGIZ   UZBEK
RUSSIAN   XIBO

KOREAN

HAN
Also:
DONGXIANG
GAOSHAN
HEZHE
HUI
LI
MANCHU
SHE
TU
TUJIA
YUGUR

TIBETAN
Also:
BAOAN
LUOBA
MENBA
QIANG
SALA

ACHANG   JINUO
BAI   LAHU
BENGLONG   LISU
BULANG   MIAO
BUYI   NAXI
DAI   NU
DONG   PUMI
DULONG   SHUI
GELAO   WA
HANI   YI
JINGPO

ZHUANG
Also:
JING
MAONAN
MULAO
YAO

The principal homelands of China's 56 ethnic peoples are indicated on this map by colour; within each area, if a group predominates, it is the first one listed. The Han, for instance, occupy most of the east, but 10 other ethnic groups also live there.

2

now routes for tourist cruises. River-boats safely carry visitors through the three main gorges—Qutang, Wuxia and Xiling—for 185 kilometres.

More than scenery enriches the south-east. Its fertile land and sub-tropical climate make it China's most important source of food. Nearly half the country's rice comes from the Yangtze and West basins, along with a profusion of other produce: peanuts and lichees, citrus fruits and sweet po-tatoes, sugar cane and tea. To these field crops must be added pigs and poultry (which live on the by-products of the fields), as well as a rich haul of seafood netted along the coast.

Rice is the staple here, and in China it is not just a single foodstuff. There are some 50,000 strains, and about a third of that number are grown in China by individual farmers. Some are valued for their taste, some for their growing properties. Fire rice, for example, can be planted in burnt-over fields, and hundred-day rice ripens earlier than others. Pearl rice has small, chewy grains, favoured in the north. Gluti-nous rice cooks into a sticky mass that is extra-filling; this is the rice that is shaped into balls. Another strain, aromatic rice, is much admired for its piquant, nutty scent (in times past, most of this costly kind of rice ended up in the imperial court).

The south-east is home to more than half the population of the country. Yet for nearly all of the history of China, the region has been subordinate to the wheat-producing north-east. "The northerner is essentially a conqueror and the southerner is essentially a trader," maintained Lin Yutang. "Of all the imperial brigands who have founded Chinese dynasties, none have come from south of the Yangtze. The

tradition developed that no rice-eating southerners could mount the dragon throne, and only noodle-eating north-erners could."

The capital city, Peking, lies in the north-eastern quadrant—essentially a flat, treeless prairie with hot, often dry, summers and long, harsh winters. The region sweeps from the fringes of the Yangtze valley north to the mountains of Heilongjiang, hard by Siberia and near the Sea of Japan. Westwards, it crosses the wind-washed steppes of Inner Mongolia, just beyond the snail's trail of the Great Wall.

On the eastern rim of the quadrant, however, lies one of the heaviest concentrations of industry in China. Iron and steel mills, oil refineries, ship-yards, electric generating plants and major factories for the production of machine tools, earth-moving equip-ment, lorries, tractors and locomotives are clustered round Peking and the shoreline of Bo Hau Gulf.

Industries grew here because ample fuel was nearby at such surface coal pits as Fuxin, China's largest. More re-cently, fuel for Chinese industry and for export has come from huge oil fields in the Songhua Jiang-Liao He basin. Oil has turned the northern village of Daqing into a boom town of refineries, petrochemical plants and 700,000 people. Pipelines running from Daqing to the port cities of Qinhuangdao and Luda carry Daqing's oil to tankers for export. Some Chinese oil goes to Hong Kong and Thailand, while Japan alone has purchased close to 10 million tonnes in a year. And the discovery in 1979 of oil under the shallow waters of the Bo Hai Gulf may increase this out-ward flow of Chinese crude oil.

Agriculture rather than industry, of course, was the foundation of the power

of the north-east quadrant. Despite its harsh and fickle climate, the vast plain around Peking, covering 324,000 square kilometres, is a very productive farming area, accounting for 20 per cent of China's agricultural land. Wheat fields and tidy villages nudge the horizon in every direction.

The fertility of this plain, flat as a table over hundreds of kilometres, is owed to a felicitous combination of wind, soil and water. The water is brought down to the plain by the Yellow River, which seems to course through Chinese history like some dual-natured dragon, at once kindly and malevolent. The river supply reaches the fields, however, only be-cause of human effort at irrigation. The total of irrigated farmland in China in-creased by a third between 1965 and 1975, bringing about half of all the country's fields under irrigation; in the wheat region, the proportion of irri-gated land is much higher than the na-tional average: 80 per cent.

The river also helps to deliver the topsoil, 75 metres thick in some places and the most fertile in China. This cov-ering originates in the uplands west of Peking. Scouring winds scrape away their soil—a porous, brownish yellow earth called loess—and blow it east-wards, filling the atmosphere with dust. During the spring in Peking, the air is so dusty people often wear surgi-cal masks when they go outdoors.

Much of the dust eventually washes into the river, which gets its name from the heavy concentration of silt it picks up—a silt content higher than any other river in the world. On the final lap of its 4,632-kilometre journey to the sea, the Yellow unloads this rich cargo of silt over the North China Plain. The price paid for this enrichment has been

FOUR CUISINES FOR SUMPTUOUS DINING

Chef Zhou DeDing holds delicacies from China's great cuisines: thousand-year-old eggs, bamboo shoots, peppers, cherries and radishes—one sculpted into a bird.

The Chinese have probably been eating well longer than any other people on earth. Cooks—"doctors of food"—were accorded a higher status than medical doctors as long ago as 2000 B.C. More than 9,000 characters in Chinese script depict some aspect of food, its preparation, or the tools necessary to enjoy it. Provincial governors visiting the capital habitually brought their chefs along with them. Even Confucius is said to have divorced his wife because of her culinary shortcomings.

Chinese cooking evolved over the years into a discipline with immutable canons. Balance is crucial, especially between rice or other starches (called *fan*) on one side, and meat and vegetables (*cai*) on the other. The mixing of contrasting flavours is another principle. The smell, colour and texture—even shape—of food are all regarded as important, for dishes are designed to appeal to all the senses *(right, above)*.

The imperatives imposed by the land have shaped cuisine. Scarcity of fuel places a premium on speed in cooking, hence the emphasis on quick stir-frying techniques and thinly sliced foods that cook rapidly. Lacking refrigeration, the Chinese developed a compensating gift for preserving food through salting, smoking, curing, crystallizing and other methods.

Most of China's grasslands are unsuited to beef and dairy cattle: as a result beef is served infrequently, while milk, cheese and other dairy products are generally absent; protein is supplied by economical fish, pigs and poultry. The imperatives of land and climate have also divided Chinese cooking into four main cuisines: the north-eastern, or Mandarin, of Peking and the Yellow River basin; the coastal, of Shanghai and its environs; the south-eastern, of Canton; and the inland south-eastern, of Sichuan.

In the south-eastern cuisine of Canton—most familiar to Westerners because so many of its practitioners emigrated to Europe and America—rice is the staple because this is rice-growing country. But there are also simple fish dishes, such as bass in a zesty sauce of fermented black beans, and a soup, thick with chewy sharks' fins. Further inland is the blazing food of Sichuan. "For some," wrote food authority Margaret Gin, "the first taste of fiery Sichuan cooking will be the last. If they reach for a glass of water to put out the fire in their mouths and throats, they'll find it's like putting out a bonfire with gasoline. The flames only leap higher. But those who do not pursue it will never discover the spectrum of flavours—sour, salty, sweet, fragrant, bitter and hot—that can be tasted all at once, and that doesn't really paralyze the palate but rather stimulates the taste buds."

The coastal area around Shanghai specializes in complex dishes of seafood and elaborately braised meats. The author Emily Hahn recalls a New Year's banquet in Shanghai that included four different kinds of pork—"red-cooked pig's knuckle, steamed pork dumplings, crisp pork-skin cracklings and roast suckling pig" —plus carp and vegetables.

In the north-east, where wheaten noodles take the place of rice, many stews, barbecues and roasts are popular. Perhaps the glory of this cuisine is Peking duck, prized for its crisp golden skin. But many other dishes are notable.

Here in the capital, magnificent court banquets in centuries past were marvels of lavish inventiveness. A stupefied English guest at an 1880 feast beheld "little plates filled with elegantly raised three and four-cornered pyramids composed of little bits of pheasant, larded geese, sausages, and so forth. Here stood plates of small oranges; there, preserved plums; and here again, almonds. There were quince seeds, chick peas, chestnuts and hazel nuts; also preserved ginger, citron, and lemon." Ragouts, soups and "strong chicken hashes" followed in relentless succession, and then "tables covered with roasted pork and birds of all sorts," carved by 10 tastefully attired servants. The imperial court may be gone, but banquets continue to mark the special occasions of a Communist state with magnificent food that is a culinary wonder of the world.

2

In the Guangxi Autonomous Region
of the south-east, near Guilin,
villagers wade to their fields across a
pond; its waters reflect the scenic
limestone formations of the area.

a repeated pattern of calamitous floods. In the past 3,000 years the Yellow has breached its banks more than 1,500 times, taking a toll of more than 10 million lives. Little wonder its alternative name is China's Sorrow.

For more than 30 centuries the people of North China have been battling the Yellow with earthen dikes. As far back as 400 B.C., the river was already flowing "above ground". Today its bottom is higher than the level of surrounding fields, and at some points on its lower reaches, its surface is even 5 metres higher, held in check by massive earthworks, as tall as a barn, that cut across the horizon like a ridge of foothills. At their base, these man-made ridges are as much as 30 metres wide; at the top, 15 metres wide, enough to accommodate a two-lane motorway, and in some stretches, railway lines.

The first of the Yellow River's dike builders was a semimythical figure called Yü the Great. Chinese schoolchildren, even today, learn about his heroic exploits. Charged with the responsibility for taming the Yellow after a terrible flood in 2297 B.C., Yü is said to have mobilized thousands of people to dredge the riverbed and dig diversion canals. The work took 13 years; during that time Yü never went home, even though he passed by his house on three occasions. When the project was completed, Yü was rewarded by being made Emperor—and the Yellow supposedly remained placid for the next 1,600 years.

By the time of the Han Dynasty, historical records document huge dike-building projects. Hundreds of thousands of workers were mobilized to excavate millions of tonnes of earth and shape it into tapering mounds. To firm the dikes, the sloping sides were lined with bundles of kaoliang, a plant with an elaborate root system. Set in the dikes with their roots facing the river, the kaoliang bundles trapped silt and kept the embankment from eroding. This conservation system is still used today, especially for mending breaks in the dikes during flooding.

But as much as the dikes have been raised, the river has risen to defeat them. In one dreadful flood in 1887, it gashed a hole 90 metres wide into the south bank of the dike near the city of Zhengzhou. In minutes, the gap widened to more than half a kilometre. Surging eastwards, the waters covered an area of 26,000 square kilometres, creating a lake the size of Lake Erie, and in the process destroying 1,500 towns and villages. "Every night," wrote a newspaper correspondent, "the sound of the winds and the waters, and the weeping and crying, cries for help, make a scene of unspeakable and cruel distress."

In the 1950s the Chinese embarked on an ambitious three-part programme to harness the Yellow once and for all. Upstream, on the loess plateau, they have planted thousands of trees to retard erosion. At sensitive points in the river, they have built spur dikes, set at angles to the main dikes, to deflect the force of the flow.

Still, China's Sorrow is not entirely tamed. A prolonged spell of rain invariably brings disaster to some settlements, as the waters find a vulnerable spot and surge through. A member of a commune in Henan described a massive effort to contain the Yellow after several days of heavy summer rains in 1970 had swelled the waters to the danger point. "By the time we reached the river," he said, "we were part of a kilometre-long procession."

He found "tens of thousands of peas-

2

Golog woman of Tibet

ants at work, throwing up a new embankment half a metre high and a metre across to raise the height of the dike. Only centimetres remained between the flood crest and the top of the old dike. Basketful by basketful of earth, the new embankment grew. The commune had come within two days' rain of a considerable disaster. Now, after five days' work and with the help of thousands of other workers, it was ahead of any possible flood danger.''

West and north of the great basins of the Yellow, Yangtze and West Rivers lies two thirds of China, land as inhospitable as any on earth. Across its sparse grasses have stormed the savage horsemen who invaded the Middle Kingdom repeatedly over the millennia. Today these regions are inhabited mainly by minorities, ethnic groups who are not Han Chinese. Only there, in the north-west and the south-west quadrants, do minorities predominate.

Since the accession of the Communist regime, government policies affect-

ing the officially designated minority peoples have vacillated between measures designed to promote assimilation and programmes that recognize and even encourage ethnic diversity. Increased literacy in the Chinese language, the breakdown of regional social and economic associations, and the mass relocation of large numbers of Han Chinese into minority areas have tended to homogenize the people and emphasize similarities rather than differences. But at the same time other

Befurred Kazak nomad

initiatives have supported the official policy guaranteeing all nationalities "freedom to use and foster the growth of their spoken and written languages, and to preserve or reform their own customs or ways''.

The central government gave semi-autonomous status to five regions that have high minority populations—Guangxi, Ningxia, Inner Mongolia, Xinjiang and Tibet. This change permitted the use of local languages in

schools and regional radio broadcasts and also established centres where cadres of minorities receive special training in administration, medicine and other fields. In recent years Chinese leaders have also taken aim at the smug contempt with which Han Chinese have traditionally viewed the "barbarians" among them. This has inspired a new official tolerance for such ethnic idiosyncrasies as the dietary preferences of the Muslims and the ceremonial regalia worn by different groups on their holidays.

The most significant concession the government has made to the minorities is to exempt them from the rigid birth control regulations that by the 1980s reduced overall population growth to only 1.4 per cent annually. Minority couples may also marry earlier than the ages officially sanctioned for the Han, normally 25 for women and 27 for men. Ironically, the birth rate among minorities has lagged behind that of the Han despite these dispensations.

The largest minority groups in the

Hui boy in Muslim cap

north-western and south-western quadrants—and the peoples with the most distinctive cultures—are the Kazaks and Uygurs in the north-west, and the Tibetans in the south-west. The first two groups are Muslim; the Tibetans practise Lamaism, a modified form of Buddhism in which homage is paid to the god-like Dalai Lama. Religion by itself would set these people apart from the rest of China. But environment and lifestyle ensure much bigger differences than religion does.

The Kazaks, Uygurs and Tibetans inhabit an almost uninhabitable landscape. The Uygurs and Kazaks are scattered over the provinces of Gansu and Xinjiang—the latter alone accounts for nearly one sixth of China's land area. It is an empty sweep of hardpan desert, interrupted by arid mountains and patches of grassland, crossed by the old Silk Road that from the first century A.D. carried Oriental commerce from Chang'an to Samarkand and then to Antioch. Natives of the area say the country has three "too manys"

Traditionally clad Dai girl from Yunnan

and three "too littles": "too many winds and too little rain, too much sand and too little grass, too many stones and too little soil."

Industry is changing this remote north-west region. Minerals have been discovered in the Tian Mountains, oil in the Dzungarian basin and coal in Ürümqi, helping to balloon the population of Ürümqi, the capital city of Xinjiang region, from 80,000 in the

Uzbek elder in turban and curled-toe boots

1940s to nearly a million in the 1980s. In and around Ürümqi are plants that produce iron, cement and textiles. But growth in the region is still limited by the "too many" and "too littles", and most Uygurs and the Kazaks still live much as they have for centuries, dependent on farming and herding.

Places to farm are scattered, limited

Kirgiz girl

to a few oases. Rainfall here never exceeds 50 centimetres a year and often drops below 25 centimetres—only slightly more than reaches the Kalahari Desert in Africa. The few feeble streams trickle into the sand or evaporate in air so dry that raindrops sometimes vanish before they hit the ground. In Lop Nur—a series of salt basins where China does its atomic testing—one stream has shifted course several times, altering the position of the lake into which it empties. When Marco Polo passed Lop Nur in the 13th century, the lake was at lat. 41°N., long. 90°E.; subsequently it was at lat. 39°N., long. 88°E.; still later it returned to its previous position.

The winters are bitterly cold in the desert and the summers hot; sudden dust storms swirl up to blot out the sky and to alter the contours of the land. Marco Polo, as he headed across the featureless dunes of the 1,450-kilometre-long Taklimakan Desert, where "not a thing to eat is to be found," re-

2

ported that, "in making this journey it is customary for travellers to keep close together. All the animals have bells on their necks so they cannot go astray. And at sleeping time a signal is put up to show the direction of the next day's march." Appropriately, Taklimakan, in the language of the Uygurs, means "once you get in you can never get out."

Just north of the Taklimakan lies the lowest, hottest place in China, the 155-metre-deep Turpan depression. Summer temperatures here have reached as high as a wilting 50°C, but Turpan—a stopping place on the old Silk Road that skirts the Tian Mountains to the north—is also an oasis. Its heat is deflected by the shade of grape arbours irrigated by underground canals tapping streams in the mountains. The canals, some of them centuries old, honeycomb the desert and are maintained through access holes that pockmark the sand.

Although the canals keep Turpan's grapes watered, the vines are threatened by subzero cold in winter and wind-driven sand for three months in spring. The winds, called black hurricanes, bury people in their homes for days—much as snowstorms maroon Swiss hamlets and Canadian farms. Recent reforestation projects, forming a shelter belt around the oasis, have reduced the danger and introduced trees into a landscape once as bereft of them as adjacent Mongolia—described as a place where you would have to walk 100 kilometres to hang yourself. The shelter belts have even allowed grape growing in Turpan to become a small industry. Today the oasis produces raisins and 20 different wines.

Some other Xinjiang oases are splendidly productive as well. In the village of Hami, two recent visitors saw in the market-place "golden-crusted breadstuffs" and "stalls filled with carrots, aubergines and several varieties of beans, including one with a pod more than 30 centimetres long and circular in shape." There were squashes in profusion, onions, juicy green peppers, celery, lettuce and cucumbers, and the superbly flavoured Hami melon, each one "branded with its grower's mark, which stands out in bold relief."

Many of the 5.4 million Uygurs, sedentary farmers, live in houses made of adobe. The interior walls and the bed—an earthen slab measuring 3 by 3.5 metres in area—are covered with multicoloured quilts.

Life is quite different for the other large group of people who inhabit the north-western quadrant, the 800,000 Kazaks. They are tent-dwelling nomads, descended from the fierce, mustachioed horsemen who used to terrorize travellers along the Silk Road. Now they are peaceable herders of sheep and goats. In the summer they drive their flocks to the upland meadows of the Tian Mountains; when the snows come, they move down to the grasslands of the steppes. Their dwellings are distinctive dome-shaped structures called yurts, which are made of felt laid over a strutwork of boughs, the whole lashed down with ropes. A yurt folds into a compact bundle that is loaded, along with an impressive assortment of household furnishings, on pack animals for the journey to a new grazing site. On arrival, it is quickly set up for family living.

Inside, a yurt is capacious yet cosy. Straw mats cover the floor, and the walls are lined with storage trunks. On the trunks are piled stacks of neatly folded quilts, used by the family for everything from upholstery to insula-

A Kazak herder's yurt, carried by a cow *(below)*, is set up by unfolding the lattice wall, tying roof supports to the wall and vent ring *(centre)*, then covering with reed screens and felt *(bottom)*.

THE YURT: A COMFORTABLE HOUSE IN A PACKLOAD

The yurt has been home to China's north-western nomads for some 3,000 years. Over that span of time, the design of this original mobile home has changed little, although today some yurts are mass-produced in factories. A felt-covered willow-latticed structure, the yurt collapses into a bundle for transport by pack animal and can be erected *(left)* in about an hour to make circular living quarters—perhaps 6 metres in diameter—that are comfortable even in the harsh climate of the steppes. As many as eight layers of felt keep in warmth during the winter months,

when the temperature outside may drop to as low as −37°C, and the felts can be rolled up in the summertime to allow breezes to blow through the lattice.

Men do much of the work of assembly and disassembly, but the women supervise the job, for the yurt is their responsibility; it is usually part of a bride's dowry.

Behind the wooden or felt door—called *ish kir mas*, "the dog shall not enter"—the spartan exterior gives way to luxury. Lavishly furnished with bright rugs and carved furniture, the yurt provides a snug home on the steppes.

Amid vivid embroidered hangings and mats, a Kazak and her two children welcome Western visitors to their yurt with food and drink. In her hand, the woman has an instant photograph just given to her by a guest.

2

tion to bedding. A wooden bedstead doubles as seating, and warmth radiates from an iron stove with a chimney snaking up through the yurt roof; on the stove, likely as not, will be a pan of sheep's milk, bubbling slowly.

The Kazaks cook over an open fire when weather permits, and much of their fare is supplied by their herds. One traveller reported that a Kazak lamb, seen playing with children earlier in the day, "had been artfully reduced to 50 or 60 shish kebabs and broth" by dinnertime. Warm goat's or sheep's milk is the typical drink, sometimes mixed with black tea and butter; and fermented mare's milk makes a popular drink that is called kumiss. Into these are dunked crisp rounds of fried unleavened bread.

Even more dependent on their herds than the Kazaks are the Tibetans, who occupy the daunting region of China's south-west quadrant, the high plateaux and frozen peaks of Tibet and Qinghai, "the roof of the world". Elevations here average 4,000 metres and crest at 7,500 metres. The air is thin, the winters fiercely cold and windy, with temperatures frequently dropping to −40°C. Even in the summer, a sudden snow squall surprises no one.

At least one group of Tibetans, the Gologs who roam the high country on the border between Tibet and Qinghai, have earned a reputation for belligerence akin to that of America's Apaches. A 19th-century French explorer who angered a band of Gologs by accusing them of horse theft was unceremoniously sewn inside a yak skin and hurled into an icy river. More recently, the Gologs—with the fierce Khampas from south-east Tibet—have been in the forefront of armed resistance to Chinese occupation. Even the name suggests contrariness: Golog in Tibetan means "head on backwards".

Although the lands of the Gologs and Khampas boast rich prairies and dense forests, most of Tibet is either rocky or covered with a thin scrub suitable only for grazing the ubiquitous yak. A type of ox with shaggy hair dropping to its hooves, this creature is a pillar of the Tibetan economy. One recent visitor noted the yak's contribution to his stay: "Yak butter in our tea, yak meat in our stew, yak whey on our plates, wonderfully pungent yak yogurt to clear our palates, yak-wool cloaks over our shoulders, yak-wool carpets at our feet—and, after lunch, rides on yaks across the yak-filled valley, perched in yak-leather saddles, pulling yak-leather reins, followed by an excursion in a yak-skin boat."

The region's minimal farmland, found mostly around Lhasa, is primarily devoted to barley, cultivated briskly during the brief five-month growing season. This staple grain is stirred into tea, moistened and rolled into edible pellets, or used for chang, a barley beer. With further distillation, chang becomes the more potent arrack. Since the 1950s, the Chinese occupation has introduced vegetables into the Tibetan diet. So alien were such foods as onions, chillies and beans that the bewildered Tibetans said the Chinese ate grass, like animals.

Tibet and Qinghai support only a small population, but in their precipitous landscapes are the headwaters of two of China's great rivers: the Yellow and the Yangtze begin their journeys to the fertile valleys of the Han from the remote south-west quadrant. In a sense, these Tibetan uplands, seen by only the most intrepid travellers, nurture the whole Chinese nation.

A snow leopard hangs across the horse of a Golog nomad. These animals, an endangered species, are hunted for their bones, used in folk remedies.

TO THE WEST, ANOTHER COUNTRY

Taken together, the Kirgiz, Uygurs and Tibetans—three of the distinctive minorities of China's Far West—constitute less than 1 per cent of the country's population. Yet even this modest proportion is a tribute to their hardihood and resourcefulness. They live in harsh mountain terrain; bleak valleys and blazing deserts that rank among the least forgiving environments on earth.

The Tibetan homeland, covering 1,221,600 square kilometres north of the Himalayas, is a huge plateau only a little less dizzying in altitude than the mountains that form its backdrop. Half of all the 3.4 million people classified by the Chinese government as Tibetan reside here; the remainder are scattered through provinces to the east. About 20 per cent of Tibetans are nomads; they usually herd yaks—docile, shaggy creatures that are impervious to the bitter cold and supply not only milk and meat but also hair for weaving tents. The remaining Tibetans are farmers. Their staple is barley, which they toast lightly, grind up, and then combine with hot tea and melted yak butter to make a dish called *tsampa*.

Tibetans follow their own variant of Buddhism, but the Uygurs and Kirgiz to the north are Muslims. The Kirgiz number only 90,000; they are nomadic herders of yaks, goats, camels, sheep and horses in the high grassy valleys of the Pamirs, the mountainous borderland between China and the Soviet Union near the northwestern corner of the Tibetan region.

From the great altitudes of the Pamirs and the Tibetan plateau, the land falls abruptly into the huge Tarim Basin of Xinjiang, mostly desert and at some points dropping below sea level. This is the home of some five million Uygurs. They too are farmers, for there are oases strewn through the arid region, and the Uygurs channel snow-melt from the surrounding mountains for use in irrigating fields of cotton, wheat, cabbage and fruit.

Silhouetted against the snow-covered slopes of 7,490-metre-high Mount Muztagata in the Pamirs, a Kirgiz horseman wends his way along the old Silk Road, the fabled route of East-West commerce over the Pamirs and across the desert beyond.

A brightly dressed Golog, a nomadic
Tibetan, milks a yak. In accordance
with Tibetan Buddhist belief, her
long hair is braided in 108 strands—
the number of sacred qualities said to
constitute an enlightened mind.

In the shadows of the Himalayas,
Lhasa, the capital of Tibet and its
holiest city, occupies a plateau 3,660
metres above sea level. Lhasa is
dominated by the Potala, a sprawling
palace that was originally built
for the Dalai Lama, the spiritual
leader of Tibetan Buddhists. Many
of the Potala's religious treasures
were plundered during China's
Cultural Revolution.

NOMADS OF THE MOUNTAIN VALLEYS

Kirgiz camel drivers lead their animals to graze in a broad meadow in the foothills of the Pamir range. Although lorries nowadays carry cargo into these once-inaccessible regions, roads are few and camel caravans still distribute goods and supplies to scattered herdsmen.

A black-booted Kirgiz sits placidly with his son in a field by the old Silk Road. The father has on a traditional fleece hat, while the boy wears the army-style cap popular all over China.

Kneeling in the mountains 3,960 metres above sea level, a Kirgiz man aligns himself towards Mecca and bows in prayer.

HOME IN THE DESERT

Clutching prayer beads, a Uygur man eases his arthritis by sitting buried to his waist in the hot sands of the Turpan Basin in the Xinjiang region. The summer temperatures there regularly reach 45°C.

Traversing a section of the Silk Road, Uygurs in a donkey cart pass the monumental remains of Gaochang, a centre of culture and commerce in the Turpan Basin area between the first and 15th centuries.

Extravagantly carved and painted, with mythological figures on top of its roof, the Summer Palace of the imperial court, on Peking's Kunming Lake, was built in 1888. But its structure—especially the roof-support brackets—follows ancient designs for resisting earthquake.

A CULTURE UNIFIED BY WRITING

The Chinese typewriter consists of a printing mechanism above a tray of type that holds about 2,000 different characters. Each character is an individual word, unique, different from all the other symbols. The typist must scan the tray of type for the character needed, then press a handle that fits the character into the printing mechanism, which strikes an impression through an inked ribbon. The machine resembles a small printing press more than it does typewriters used in the West, and its operation is cumbersome and slow; the very best typists can average only 20 characters a minute, as opposed to the 80-word-a-minute rate of a very good English-language typist. The standard tray of Chinese type contains the 2,000 characters used most often, but in order to copy even an ordinary manuscript the typist must resort to extra trays holding some 9,000 more.

The origins of this stenographic problem are ancient: specimens of Chinese writing date from as early as 2000 B.C., and the essential classic form had been fixed by 1200 B.C. Prodigality is built into it. Most European languages employ only 26 letters to represent all spoken sounds; the Chinese written language, by contrast, is a storehouse with more than 50,000 different characters, each standing for a different word.

Daunting feats of memory are required to master such a language. A child must be able to recognize more than 1,000 separate characters before being able to read even simple texts. Yet there are advantages to such a system of notation. It has long been, and remains today, a powerful force for cultural and political unity. People in China's various regions are actually a mix of diverse ethnic origins, and they speak mutually unintelligible dialects, yet all can read the same language, just as anyone in any country, no matter what the native tongue, can read Arabic numerals. The numeral 2 has the same meaning to natives of Germany, France and Spain, although they spell it as *zwei*, *deux* and *dos*.

Because all literate Chinese, whatever dialect they have spoken, have been able to read the same books, they have felt themselves part of a single, venerable, ongoing world. The written language not only gave the Chinese a common culture, it also helped to define that culture to an unusual extent. The Chinese term for civilization, *wenhua*, noted one scholar, means "the transforming influence of writing".

Independent of any pronunciation changes, the writing perpetuated traditional ideas and forms by keeping classic works understandable millennium after millennium. Thus it embedded certain philosophical ideas in the minds of all the elite, and established certain ideals of individual behaviour, family relations and government organization. Its subtle complexities lent unique distinction to poetry, which became the most admired literary form. In past centuries any man worthy of respect had to display high literary talent. (Until recent times, women in China were expected to excel in the domestic arts and were excluded from all others. They were allowed no role in the nation's public or political life.)

Because the key to power and influence was the written language rather than the spoken, the mechanics of writing—the appearance of the characters—became very important. Thus an individual was judged not only by the content of writing, but also by the quality of the brush-and-ink calligraphy, that gave form to the content. Calligraphy, in fact, became the basis for Chinese painting, which, unlike the art of the West, depends less on the modelling of light and shadows than on linear images created by incredibly delicate brushstrokes.

The culture based on writing—philosophy, poetry and painting—has been so closely associated with positions of authority, that it has won the highest respect from the Chinese. Secondary in their minds have been other intellectual and artistic endeavours much admired by Westerners. Delicate and colourful pottery, superb sculptures in bronze and clay, spectacular theatrical shows—and scientific and technological feats such as the inventions of gunpowder, rockets, clocks and printing—were to the Chinese all craftwork, and so com-mendable, perhaps, but not to be compared with poetry or philosophy.

The philosophies that guided Chinese life until the Communist takeover are very old ones, and the extreme age of the written language enables the Chinese of today to be in direct touch with these ethical foundations. Though only very well-educated Chinese now read the ancient classics, all modern Chinese are familiar with the ideas attributed to the sages Confucius and Lao Zi, which spell out moral precepts and views of life that have influenced Chinese thinking and behaviour for more than 2,000 years.

Confucius was born, it is said, in 551 B.C. in what is now Shandong province. Living in a time when China was divided into a number of belligerent feudal states, he became a wandering scholar, visiting the courts of several rulers and attempting to preach honesty and moderation to men more interested in bloodshed and plunder. He supposedly lived to the age of 72, but failed to effect any of the reforms that he believed would bring order out of the chaos of his day. Many contemporaries thought him an officious windbag, and his own writings—if any—were neglected and thereby lost.

Confucius had attracted some disciples, however, and about a century and a half after his death several students of these disciples put together a collection, called the *Analects*, of what purported to be the master's thoughts. How accurately this work represents Confucius' own teachings is uncertain, but it provided the basis for what came to be considered Confucianism. Although fragmentary and hardly consistent, the *Analects* presents several significant themes. Confucianism held that people should be content with their station in life. It maintained the importance of tradition, of obedience to authority, of rites and etiquette in the regulation of daily life, and of a rational, benevolent existence. Equally important is a view of the state as simply the family writ large. The Emperor was supposed to act the part of a loving, concerned father, and the subjects his loyal, respectful children.

For these reasons, Confucianism was the ethical system favoured by China's rulers; it teaches obedience to higher authority. The second paragraph of the *Analects* reads: "Those who in private life behave well towards their parents and elder brothers, in public life seldom show a disposition to resist the authority of their superiors. And as for such men starting a revolution, no instance of it has ever occurred."

Thus Confucianism is more political and practical than spiritual or metaphysical. It offers very specific proposals about how to live and how to rule the state; the *Analects* is much closer to Plato's *Republic* than to the Gospels.

Confucianism seems to be somewhat convention-bound and repressive, especially when it is compared with

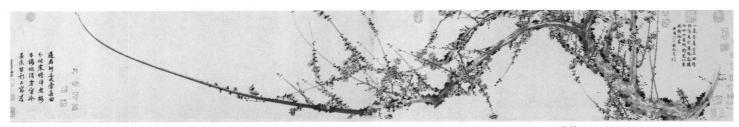

Like most Chinese paintings, this 14th-century scroll creates its effect with deft brushwork both in the image and in related poetry—here a plum branch (*detail on the right*) and verses recalling spring. The seals—called chops—identify owners.

Daoism, the other main current of Chinese culture. Any system as rigid as Confucianism always gives rise to its opposite, and in China, Daoist nature worship is that alternative.

The founder of Daoism, Lao Zi, is said to have lived in the sixth century B.C. So little is known about him that he long ago became the subject of fantastic legends. According to one tale, he was conceived on a clear night in 666 B.C. when his mother was thrilled by the beauty of a falling star. A 62-year pregnancy followed. When at last the child was born, he had white hair and was able to speak; the name of Lao Zi means "Old Master". Tradition holds that he then lived 110 years, devoting many of them to keeping the archives of the Zhou Dynasty. At last, repelled by the sordidness of the human condition, he left the Zhou court, jotting down the *Dao De Jing, The Classic of the Way and Its Power*, shortly before his death.

The way in question is the rhythm of the cosmos; the power is the vigour and capacity acquired by an individual attuned to this rhythm. Daoism, unlike Confucianism, is private rather than public, passive rather than active, witty rather than moralistic, mystical rather than commonsensical. It espouses the simple life of the villager or hermit, of a poetic soul who has put aside worldly affairs to seek unity with nature. A celebrated Daoist story of such attunement tells of Zhuang Zi, one of the early Daoist philosophers (369-286 B.C.), who once dreamt that he was a butterfly: "Suddenly he woke and found to his astonishment that he was Zhuang Zi. But it was hard to be sure whether he really was Zhuang Zi and had only dreamt that he was a butterfly, or was really a butterfly and was only dreaming he was Zhuang Zi."

In dismissing worldly ambition, the *Dao De Jing* admonishes, "There is no

3

guilt greater than to sanction ambition, no calamity greater than to be discontented with one's lot, no fault greater than the wish to be getting.'' Thus Daoism speaks to one side of the human character, appealing to the desire for quiet contemplation of beauty and for separation from the demands of the world. Confucianism speaks to the other side—obedience to the needs of family and society, to duty, to everyday responsibilities. A man holding an important job or government post tends to be a Confucian, a Chinese commentator once noted, while a man out of office is a Daoist.

Both Confucianism and Daoism are essentially ethical systems rather than religions. Neither one posits an omnipotent God—although Daoism over the centuries came to incorporate a large number of folk deities such as Zao Wang, the Lord of the Stove, who, if properly propitiated, brought good fortune to hearth and home. Neither system speaks of a hereafter. This need was supplied by Buddhism, which travelled from India, the land of its birth, to China in the first century A.D. According to Buddhism's founder, a noble named Siddhartha Gautama, a soul purified of worldly desires by abstinence and contemplation could achieve eternal peace, or Nirvana.

The new faith fitted comfortably with Daoism, which also recommended contemplation and removal from the everyday world, and it did not contradict the Confucian ideal of moderation and self-control. Since none of the three claimed exclusive possession of the Truth—as, for example, do Islam and Christianity—they could coexist in the same nation, or in the same human mind. So while millions of Chinese over the centuries embraced

Buddhist mysticism, millions more observed Buddhist rituals—in ornate temples and monasteries—while at the same time believing in following the complementary wisdom of Daoist and Confucian writings.

This Chinese hospitality to different systems of thought and belief was seen at the very pinnacle of the state: a number of Emperors were Buddhists, even though Confucianism was the official state doctrine. Indeed, a thorough knowledge of the Confucian classics came to be the essential qualification for government employment. For nearly 1,400 years, from the sixth century, the huge bureaucracy ruling China was recruited through examinations testing the applicants' mastery of Confucian canon.

Although acceptance into the civil service was based on individual merit, an advantage lay, of course, with sons of the wealthy, whose parents could afford to finance the necessary study. It took many years for a youth to learn the difficult written language, to develop a fine hand at calligraphy and above all to memorize the Confucian literature and a handful of other classic books as well. Even so, the examinations were open to any man, regardless of birth, and on occasion an entire village would band together to sponsor the education of an unusually bright farm boy.

The prestige that was instantly conferred on a man who passed the examinations was tremendous. One 18th-century novel tells of Fan Jin, a 54-year-old candidate for the official examinations who failed so many times in 34 years of trying that he ends up as a "white-bearded and extremely skinny man with a worn-out felt hat". A pauper who is not able to feed his wife and his aged mother, he is despised by

Four room-mates study in their cluttered room with a prized tool, a Japanese calculator, within reach.

Intent students listen to a physics lecture; among them is one enrolled from a foreign country *(centre, right)*.

students sleep beyond 6.30, since at that hour loudspeakers on campus begin blaring a half hour of national news. "You can't turn it off," one student commented, "and it makes a lot of noise."

Breakfast, which consists of steamed bread or thin rice gruel spiced by pickled vegetables, follows at 7 o'clock. At 7.30 the first class begins. Classes last 50 minutes each, with a 10-minute break in between. After the first two classes of the day are over, the campus-wide public address system comes on again with a national, standardized exercise programme, complete with instructions and upbeat music. The calisthenics are very popular; students, teachers and even elderly passers-by stop to go through the routine.

Soon after the loudspeakers fall silent, the treadmill of successive

A woman student trains on a lathe in the machine shop.

A student practises computer programming.

The lunchtime break at 11.30 provides the most relaxed part of the Qinghua student's day. The staple in the university cafeteria, which serves 1,000 meals a day, is rice or bread, with a dish of meat or vegetables—perhaps tomatoes stir fried with eggs, or chopped meat and potatoes. A favourite dish is fish fried in sugar and vinegar, but that vanishes swiftly. "If you are 10 minutes late," said a student, "it's all gone."

Ration coupons are required for many foods and even for the oil the foods are cooked in. Each student is allowed only seven catties (about 3.5 kilograms) of rice each month and 12 catties of flour products. Students must also furnish their own eating utensils because the cafeteria does not provide any, and they must wash them afterwards in a communal washroom that lacks

class periods resumes. At Qinghua most of these periods consist of lectures in packed rooms on such subjects as chemical or agricultural engineering. The classes are pervaded by a deadly seriousness that can be seen reflected in the faces of the students, who may include some from other countries, mostly Third World nations.

Qinghua's daylong grind of lectures and study sessions is broken by periods in the university's cavernous shop, where students gain practical experience working with basic machine tools such as the lathe shown on the left. They also learn the use of another tool, one which has become a vital adjunct to every technical course, the computer *(above)*.

Although many of Qinghua's computers come from Japan, the scientific books and journals favoured by the students are largely British and American *(right)*. Many Chinese learn at least the rudiments of English, and they prefer to labour through the original version of a text, even if it has been translated into their own language. "The Chinese version," one student noted bluntly, "is often full of errors."

At a book sale, English-language books and journals crowd the table.

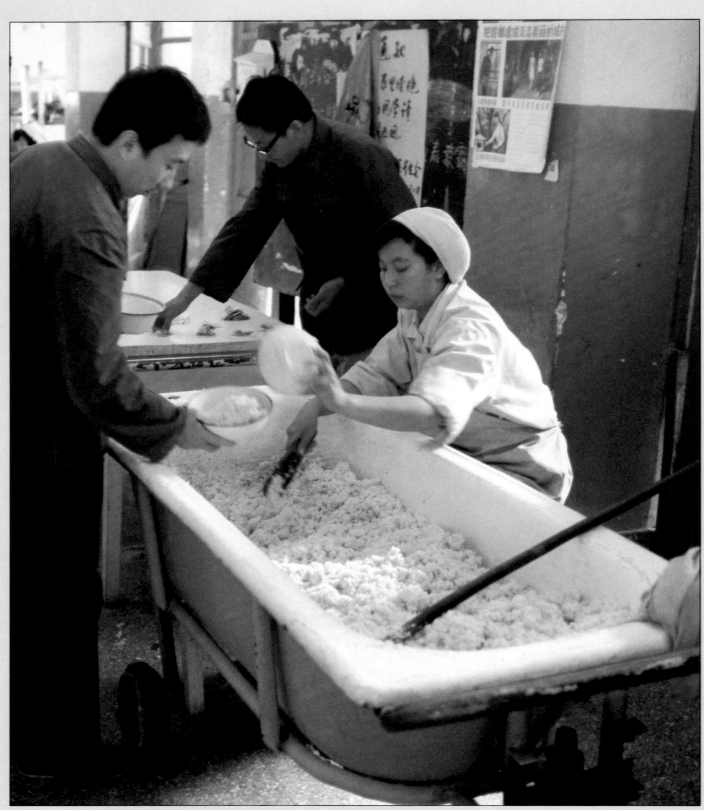

A cook ladles rice from an old bath while, next to her, a clerk counts ration coupons.

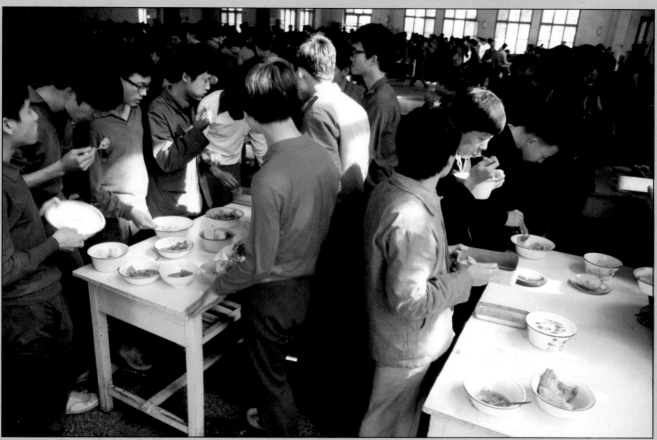

Eating standing up is the rule; there are tables but no chairs in the cafeteria.

A sun-dappled courtyard provides an alternative dining area.

both hot water and detergent. "It's all right, though," a student said, "because there's not much oil in the food."

Qinghua's long, busy day ends when the last class is over at 6.20. Supper is served promptly at 6.30. It is much like lunch, except that students can buy food left over from the noon meal at discount prices. The cost of meals is virtually the only expense the students have; the state pays for their tuition, accommodation and medical care. Indeed, those students who held jobs before entering a university are paid their regular wages.

Despite the spare, regimented existence, few students at Qinghua University complain, because they know that the chance to acquire an advanced education is a rare privilege. To get in, they must pass a stringent

Under an ancient tree, two students hold hands.

national entrance examination. Given each July, it lasts three days, and only about 10 per cent of all candidates are successful. Moreover, just a small fraction of the brightest young people are even allowed to sit for the test. As a result, about 3 per cent of China's college-age population attends an institution of higher learning, compared with 23 per cent in the Soviet Union and 35 per cent in the United States.

University life is not a ceaseless grind. There are moments of free time—between classes, on Sundays (classes are held as usual on Saturdays) or after supper in the evening. Many students participate in sports: Qinghua provides equipment for friendly matches of soccer, basketball and volleyball. Others, like the couple on the left, simply seek a bench in a quiet corner of the campus and, in the immemorial fashion of students everywhere, talk of more intimate matters than lathes or computers.

his father-in-law, Hu the butcher.

When Fan at last passes the prefectural examinations and asks Hu for travelling money so that he can take the crucial provincial examinations, Hu denounces him: "Do you know the reason you passed the last examination? It had nothing to do with your writing, which was bad; it was because the examiner felt sorry because of your advanced age. You passed because of his charity; do you understand?"

The butcher continues to berate the unfortunate Fan, comparing him unkindly to sons of the neighbouring Zhang family who have passed the examinations. "Each of them is a millionaire and all of them have round faces and large ears. Look at you: you have a pointed mouth and a chin like a monkey's. If I were you, I would forget about taking more examinations."

Nonetheless the much-abused Fan somehow manages to take the provincial examinations. When he discovers that he has passed with a high score and is now eligible for a lucrative government office, he faints and then goes mad. He stumbles into a muddy pond and wanders about the village, laughing and clapping his hands.

Fan is restored to his senses only when Hu, suppressing the awe that he now feels for his brilliant son-in-law, pretends to berate him in the usual manner and slaps him in the face. As the story comes to an end, the triumphant butcher announces to the townspeople that he need never slaughter another pig, for with Fan in the family its future is secure. "As far as I can see, my livelihood has been assured for the rest of my life. I often say that my son-in-law is not only scholarly and wise but also unusually handsome. How can those members of the Zhang

family be compared with him, who is infinitely better-looking?"

The civil service examination system survived into the first years of the 20th century. In *China Men*, the contemporary Chinese-American writer Maxine Hong Kingston relates how her father, born into a peasant family in China during the last years of the Empire, was considered from infancy to be a possible candidate for high office. His mother, certain that his long fingers meant he was destined to hold a writing brush, gave him the Four Treasures of the Study—ink, inkslab, paper and brush. Even before the baby was able to talk, itinerant scholars were persuaded to draw giant characters for him and hold them up over his crib.

When the boy (whom Maxine Kingston referred to as Ba Ba, "father") was 14 years old, he took the qualifying test for the last imperial examination ever given: "An official led Ba Ba to a cell, where he asked him to undress. The official looked over his naked body for notes written on the skin, combed through his long hair for hidden papers, cut open the seams and hems of his clothes." Ba Ba was kept in a cell until dawn, when he was led to the testing room for the oral examination that preceded the written tests. "Ba Ba stood with his face to the wall and his hands clasped behind him. In this position he recited by heart from the Three Character Classics, the Five Classics and the Thirteen Classics by Confucius' disciples." When this oral test was over he wrote for three days poems and essays in a variety of styles and in different kinds of calligraphy. Yet after all that, he scored only well enough to become a schoolteacher.

Soon after Maxine Kingston's father emerged from this ordeal, the entire

3

traditional educational system was swept away, to be replaced with one based on European models: today both boys and girls receive six years of primary school, six years of middle school and, for the gifted and fortunate, four or five years of university *(pages 70–77)*. Most university students specialize narrowly in technical subjects. In the old days such specialization in practical subject matter was secondary to the mastery of the classics. Every scholar memorized the same texts, understood the same allusions and practised the same arts, all of them derived from writing. Of these traditional arts, philosophy might be valued as the basis for a career in government, but poetry ranked highest as an aesthetically rewarding and intellectually demanding endeavour.

The Chinese system of characters is well-suited to poetry for a number of reasons. Many characters are pungently rich in acquired associations, as though each had been steeped in the brew of the accumulated centuries. At the same time, written Chinese is a wonderfully concrete medium. Consider the word for "way" or "path", for instance. This character is one of the most venerable in the language—the *dao* in Daoism. At the same time, the character contains within it a pictorial element resembling a foot striding forwards—a vigorous rendering of the otherwise vague notion of a path.

Many thousands of characters possess the same sort of visual vitality. A good number look like what they mean. Others are vivid metaphorical representations of abstract qualities. "Peace", for example, is unforgettably rendered by an image of domestic tranquillity, a woman under a roof. The written language is thus terse and vivid and it lends Chinese poetry a swift economy unattainable in languages using phonetic systems.

The greatest Chinese poetry was written during the Tang and Song periods. Among the poets ranked most highly were Li Bai *(701–762)*, Du Fu *(712–770)* and Bai Juyi *(772–846)*.

Li Bai was a rebel and in many ways a wastrel. An enthusiastic drinker and womanizer, he had driven away his wife and their children by the time that he was 30 years old. Undismayed, Li Bai joined a fellowship devoted to wine and song; the group was known as the Six Idlers of the Bamboo Valley. After a Daoist scholar lured him to the Tang capital city of Chang'an, Li Bai took up with an equally jovial society there, the Eight Immortals of the Wine Cup. A glimpse of Li Bai during this period is found in a description that was written by his friend Du Fu:

As for Li Bai, give him a jugful,
He will write one hundred poems.
He drowses in a wine-shop
On a city street of Chang'an;
And though his sovereign calls,
He will not board the imperial barge.
"Please your Majesty," says he,
"I am a god of wine."

Many of Li Bai's own verses celebrate the virtues of drink and they bear titles such as "Drinking Alone by Moonlight" or "Waking from Drunkenness on a Spring Day". Here is one of his poems, "Self-Abandonment", in its entirety:

I sat drinking and did not notice the dusk,
Till falling petals filled the folds of my dress.
Drunken I rose and walked to the moonlit
* stream;*
The birds were gone, and the men also few.

But Li Bai's talent is perhaps best seen in his masterful exploitation of the brevity that makes Chinese poetry so different from the great classic poems of the West, such as the book-length *Iliad* of Homer. In just four lines, Li Bai expressed "Night Thoughts":

Bright shines the moonlight at the foot of my
* bed,*
Perhaps reflected from frost on the ground.
Lifting my head I gaze at the bright moon,
Bowing my head I think of my family home.

When Li Bai was 45, the Tang Emperor Ming Huang, a great patron of the arts, allowed his unruly pet poet to leave the imperial court. Li Bai then became a vagabond, idling along the roads, drinking and writing verse. He finally reached Anhui province, where he died, according to legend, in his cups: he attempted to embrace the reflection of the moon in a river and he drowned.

Li Bai's friend Du Fu also stood outside the rigid system of the Confucian state. He had difficulty in passing the state examinations and never rose high in the government, perhaps because he had an unusually sensitive conscience for his period and deplored the effects of war and imperial extravagance on the lives of the poor. In one poem he contrasts imperial decadence with the poverty outside the court:

Behind the red-lacquered gate, wine is left to
* sour, meat to rot.*
Outside these gates lie the bones of the frozen
* and the starved.*
The flourishing and the withered are just a
* foot apart—*
It rends my heart to ponder it.

The third genius of Tang poetry, Bai

BRIGHT PAINTINGS FROM THE PEASANT ARTISTS OF JINSHAN

In a work done by a tractor driver, saleswomen show pottery to customers.

Yuan Sidi, who took up painting in her seventies, finishes one of her flower paintings. Behind her is another one.

The White Snake surprises her husband *(background)* in a boldly painted bedroom.

These brightly coloured paintings, startlingly different from the classic Chinese art admired the world over *(pages 68–69)*, are nonetheless typically Chinese. Created by peasants of Jinshan, near Shanghai, they combine objects from different times and places as seen from different perspectives, a style that can be traced back to painted pottery produced in China during neolithic times.

Folk painting was originally encouraged by the Communists for ideological purposes—"carrying on the revolutionary struggle through the masses' own art". But recent works have been apolitical, depicting everyday scenes such as shop interiors *(above, left)* or illustrating folk tales such as the story of the White Snake *(left)*, in which a serpent turns into a woman, then back into a snake.

Juyi, was, unlike his colleagues, a committed Confucian scholar; although he deprecated his achievements, he became a respected bureaucrat. At the age of 28 he passed the state examinations with honour:

For ten years I never left my books;
I went up and won unmerited praise.
My high place I do not much prize;
The joy of my parents will first make me
* proud.*

As a young official, Bai Juyi encountered difficulties when he was too quick to speak out against what he considered to be misguided official policy; he was banished for five years. Eventually he was reprieved, however, and he rose to be appointed governor first of Hangzhou and then, at the age of 53, of Suzhou.

Despite these successes, Bai Juyi's real triumph was the great popularity that he won as a poet during his lifetime. His poems were inscribed on the walls of village schools and were memorized by princes, peasants, and even prostitutes. One dancing girl is said to have declared to a client, "You must not think I'm an ordinary dancing girl. I can recite Master Bai's 'Everlasting Wrong'"—and she promptly raised her price.

Bai Juyi's popularity was due in part to his simplicity of language. He said that he used to read his poems to an elderly peasant woman and that he would then strike out any expression that she was not able to understand. As a loyal Confucian, Bai advanced the theory that the only function of poetry is moral instruction; fortunately, Bai's verse often belies this didacticism and instead expresses his observant response to nature. In the year 818 he wrote of his first sight of the great gorges of the Yangtze River:

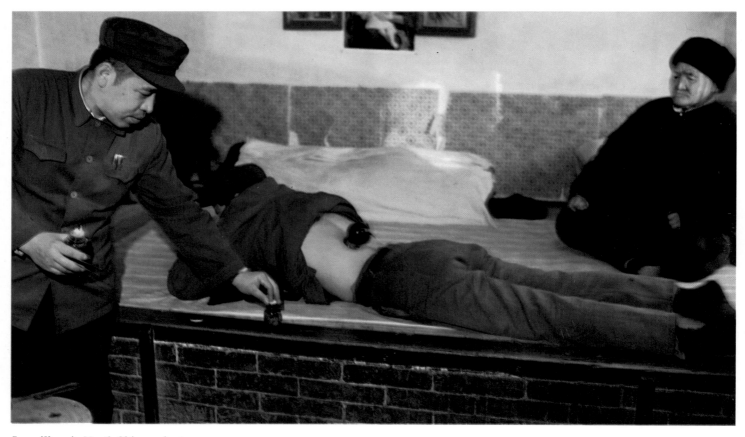

In a village in North China, a doctor trained both in modern Western and in traditional medicine treats a patient by the ancient technique of cupping. The cups are heated and then placed on the patient's skin; they are supposed to draw out disease.

Above, a mountain ten thousand feet high:
Below, a river a thousand fathoms deep.
A strip of green, walled by cliffs of stone,
Wide enough for the passage of a single reed.
At Jutang a straight cleft yawns:
At Yenyu islands block the stream.
Long before night the walls are black with
* dusk;*
Without wind white waves rise.
The big rocks are like a flat sword:
The little rocks resemble ivory tusks.

In China, the beauty of thought and expression in a poem was hardly more honoured than the beauty of its written characters. The way a master calligrapher wielded his brush was a window into the soul, a direct expression of taste, skill and refinement. The choice of paper, ink, brush and style of script—from among several distinct styles—were all taken not only as aesthetic but also as moral decisions.

No two masters wrote alike; their letters were as personal as their fingerprints, and as inimitable. Connoisseurs studied the texts of masters to admire the vitality of the characters, their shapes and spacing. Fine calligraphy matched to well-chosen phrases carried extra persuasive power. An old story tells of a general who surrendered his army simply because the enemy commander's note demanding capitulation was so elegantly phrased and beautifully rendered that it could not be refused.

So passionate a matter was calligraphy that some Chinese collectors would resort to almost any stratagems to secure fine texts, such as those done by the most famous calligrapher in all Chinese history, Wang Xizhi (321–379). His writing of a preface to a group of poems called *The Orchid Pavillion* is considered the supreme example of the art. It was Wang who spoke of calligraphy in mystical terms drawn from nature. "Every horizontal stroke is like a mass of clouds in battle formation, every hook like a bent bow of the greatest strength, every dot like a falling rock from a high peak."

Three centuries after *The Orchid Pavillion* was written, Wang's scroll came into the possession of a Buddhist monk. The Emperor sought in vain to procure it from the monk and at last sent an envoy to steal it. Posing as a student, the envoy won the confidence of the monk, who one day went out and carelessly left his prized possession unguarded. The faithless student instantly discarded his mendicant's rags, donned his imperial uniform and sped back to the capital with *The Orchid Pavillion* concealed in the gown's capacious sleeve. According to the story, the monk so mourned his loss that he died before the year was out.

The brushstrokes of the finest calligraphy set the pattern for Chinese paintings, many of which include written poems. By the fifth century, painting had been defined in six canons by Xie He, an influential critic. His rules required likenesses, versatile colours, planned representation of space, faithfulness to tradition and lifelike spirit. But his first rule was deft brushstrokes. They were, said one commentator, the artist's "heartprint"; another likened them to "a flock of birds darting out of the forest, or a frightened snake disappearing in the grass, or the cracks in a shattered wall".

The six canons of Xie He governed painting for almost a thousand years, although the stipulations for brushwork were perhaps the only ones followed exactly. Slavish imitation of the real world was decried, and many artists concentrated more on expressing the spirit of the subject than on copying its form.

In accordance with the canons of scholarly "civilized" taste, minimalist landscapes were regarded as the ideal medium for allusion to past masters and aesthetic contemplation. No attempt was made to create a sense of perspective by the Western "vanishing point" technique, which presents a view as if seen through a window. Instead, the Chinese artists indicated space and distance by the choice of colour, the blurring of outlines and the use of overlapping images of different heights.

These techniques were brought to a high level during the Tang and Song Dynasties. One of the outstanding artists of the Tang period was Wu Daozi (700-760), who was renowned for the amazing speed with which he was able to complete his frescoes on the walls of the Buddhist temples. When the people of the capital city of Chang'an heard that Wu Daozi was going to add the haloes to several sacred Buddhist figures that he had previously painted, hundreds of people crowded round to watch him do it. "He executed the haloes with so violent a rush and swirl," one of the townsmen recalled, "that it seemed as though a whirlwind possessed his hand, and all who saw it cried that some god was helping him."

In Song times, painting was "the finest embodiment of the Song genius," wrote the art historian Hugo Munsterberg. "It is the landscape painting of the Song period which in the eyes of most critics is the supreme achievement of Chinese art."

Many Song Dynasty landscapes were painted on a silk or paper scroll

MASTERPIECES IN PORCELAIN FROM FIVE DYNASTIES

Chinese potters discovered how to make porcelain in the ninth century, during the Tang Dynasty. The secret: add rock minerals to a fine clay called kaolin and fire pieces made from the mixture at very high temperatures—above 1,200°C. The result was the finest of all ceramics—hard, thin, translucent and able to take the most brilliant colours.

The best of early Chinese porcelains were white *(below, left)*, but during the Yuan Dynasty (1279–1368) the artisans began to add ornate designs, using a breathtakingly deep blue pigment made from cobalt. Potters of the Ming era (1368–1644) perfected this blue-and-white porcelain; later artists of the Qing Dynasty (1644–1912) employed colours that were derived from gold to produce a variety of shades of rose.

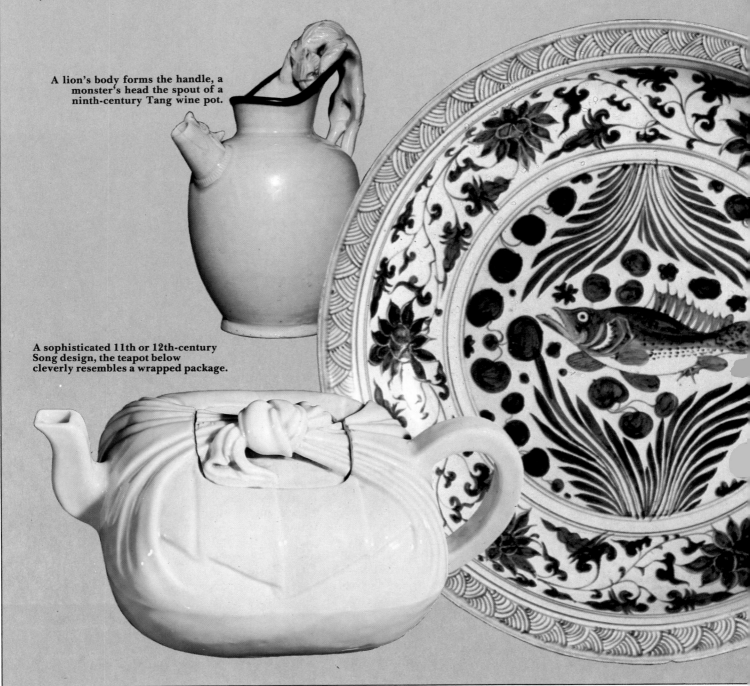

A lion's body forms the handle, a monster's head the spout of a ninth-century Tang wine pot.

A sophisticated 11th or 12th-century Song design, the teapot below cleverly resembles a wrapped package.

Subtle shadings of rose make the peaches on this 18th-century Qing vase appear round.

Intricate floral shapes interlink on the delicately coloured 15th-century Ming vase below.

A 14th-century Yuan plate shows the bold, exuberant designs and deep blue underglaze typical of the era.

about 2 metres long and more than 30 centimetres wide. They were meant to be unrolled slowly so that no more than 60 centimetres was visible at any one time, the better to display the fine details and exquisite brushwork. The scrolls generally depict gnat-sized travellers who are walking along a river or through a gorge against a backdrop of towering mist-shrouded mountains.

These images convey the insignificance of humanity in comparison with the vastness and grandeur of nature. Human beings and all their works—travellers, tiny fishermen who seine the waters with a net, spiderweb bridges, microscopically detailed monasteries—are dwarfed by plunging waterfalls and sheer mountain faces. This sense of spaciousness is heightened by the narrative quality of many scrolls. The scenes, viewed in succession, often show the characters at different moments in their travels, and thus mankind is seen wandering through time as well as space. "Human eyes are limited," said one early master, "yet with one small brush I can draw the vast universe."

Any culture as refined and elegant as the Chinese was bound to be remarkable not only for its high intellectual arts, but also for its decorative wares, and indeed artisans of many dynasties excelled in carving jade, lacquering furniture and embroidering silk. In addition, they made the first true porcelain, creating objects of unprecedented translucence, resonance and thinness *(pages 82–83)*. There were thousands of kilns all over China during the Song, and potters jealously guarded their formulae and techniques. Daughters were not allowed to learn the family's secret techniques lest, on marrying and leaving the family, they should take the

Dazzling costumes like the ones in the scene above are integral to traditional Peking Opera. Most performances, based on romantic legends, combine singing, dance, acrobatics and mime—so stylized that there are 50 ways of moving a sleeve, each with its own meaning.

tricks of the trade with them.

Sculpture, like pottery making, was considered more a craft than a high art in traditional China, although today many of these works are considered masterpieces. Some of the best Chinese sculptures were Buddhist cult images, made for temples or private worship. During the turbulent fourth to sixth centuries, newly converted Emperors ordered huge images of the Buddha, as tall as 16 metres, to be carved out of living rock. At Yungang in Shanxi province west of Peking, sculptors worked for 40 years filling caves with Buddhist images. Many generations of sculptors also worked on a huge Buddhist shrine called Dunhuang, in Gansu province. There, over a period of 15 centuries, from 366 to the waning days of the Empire early in the 20th century, they filled a series of caves with countless Buddhist sculptures of surpassing calm and elegance.

However, the most astonishing Chinese sculptures are those recovered from graves, clay figures that provide matchless records of the peoples of various dynasties. For example, Emperor Shi Huang Di of the Qin Dynasty, who died in 210 B.C., was surrounded in death by life-sized representations of his army arranged in formation—at least 7,500 figures.

Smaller but brightly coloured figurines from graves of the Tang Dynasty reveal the cosmopolitan society of that period, portraying foreign traders such as Turks, Arabs, Jews and Africans, exotic animals such as double-humped Bactrian camels, tigers and Arabian horses, and Chinese dancers, grooms and merchants *(pages 86–87)*.

These glimpses into everyday life reveal flourishing popular arts. By the time of the Song Dynasty, folk artists had perfected the use of rag paper for fashioning decorative lanterns, kites and umbrellas. Woodblock prints were produced in enormous quantities; they were hung in virtually every Chinese house as good-luck charms. Other folk arts such as embroidery, paper cutouts and even painting thrived—and they continue to be practised to this day *(page 79)*.

Such lively folk arts aside, Chinese culture throughout its very long history was essentially elitist. The literate intelligentsia formed a small proportion of the population, and this privileged elite produced many of China's finest poems, paintings and other works of art. The imperial court, its coterie and the scholarly Confucian bureaucracy held, in effect, a monopoly on high culture.

This elitist culture began to disintegrate soon after the fall of the Empire. Students demonstrated to bring an end to the rigid Confucian education, which could not prepare leaders to cope with the 20th-century world. By 1919 a simpler style of writing, closer to speech, began to replace the traditional literary language—which was quite different from spoken Chinese. Soon after the Communist takeover in 1949, the written characters themselves were simplified to make them less difficult to inscribe and memorize. Although the new characters are less elegant than those of classic calligraphy, the simplification greatly aided education and helped so many illiterate adults to learn to read that the nation's literacy rate jumped from 15 per cent to more than 75 per cent within one generation.

The Communists moved not only to change the classic calligraphy, but also to downgrade all traditional arts.

Elitist culture was, of course, anathema to them. Under Mao, and especially during the Great Proletarian Cultural Revolution that raged from 1966 to 1976 *(Chapter 5)*, official policy was unremittingly hostile to China's past. Although Mao was himself schooled as a classical poet, he deplored the elitism of the past and called for art to serve the revolution. At the height of the Cultural Revolution's hysteria, museums were closed, art schools were shuttered and many writers, painters and performers were imprisoned. Confucius was denounced as "a stinking corpse" and "the spokesman for the decadent slave-owning aristocracy".

This assault on the arts came to an end shortly after Mao's death. New paintings that used traditional modes of brush and ink began to appear, although in the mist-shrouded mountains could now be seen glimpses of red flags and power lines. A historical ballet based on Buddhist frescoes from Dunhuang and called *Along the Silk Road* was staged. Similarly, plays and operas on historic themes were revived, and stories picturing the sufferings of people during the Cultural Revolution were published (this new writing was called the "literature of the wounded"). Even Confucius staged something of a come-back. His teachings were once again studied, and public slogans called for a revival of such virtues as courtesy, morality, hygiene and purity of soul, restoring to Chinese culture its traditional values.

Youth, third or fourth century B.C.

Bronze lantern, second centur

Imperial warrior, third century B.C.

A LEGACY OF LIFELIKE SCULPTURE

Sculpture was considered a secondary art in traditional China, but a multitude of surviving examples testifies to its excellence. The land is dotted with many thousands of statues of animals and Buddhas—some astonishingly large *(pages 14–15)*. And in recent decades archaeologists have found a wealth of buried works fabricated by gifted—if anonymous—artists.

The earliest Chinese bronze sculptures were stylized bas-reliefs of real beasts or fabulous monsters; these works usually adorned bronze vessels, and their quality is unsurpassed to this day. Later, about the third century B.C., Chinese bronze-workers began to fashion more realistic figures like the superb bronze statue on the far left; only 29 centimetres tall, it depicts a boy holding two jade birds. The other sculptures on these pages represent 1,000 years of lifelike representations of beasts and humans, many done in ceramic rather than bronze.

A triumph of this realism is the life-sized terracotta soldier opposite, armoured for combat and ready to draw a now-vanished bow. Thousands of such martial figures have been found in the huge underground tomb of the first Qin Emperor, Shi Huang Di. Not only realistic but also utilitarian is the somewhat later bronze of a servant holding a lamp. The lamp housed a candle; the right sleeve served as a flue, and the body trapped the candle smoke.

Among the most famous of Chinese sculptures are figures of animals, such as the graceful horse below. It and the kneeling camel were discovered in tombs of the wealthy elite, many of whom profited from trade caravans to India and the Near East in the Sui and Tang Dynasties.

Saddle horse, eighth century.

Bactrian camel, sixth century.

Iron-willed Empress Dowager Ci Xi is
supported by ladies-in-waiting for a
1903 portrait. Shrewd but short-sighted,
the former concubine controlled
the dying Chinese Empire for half a
century, blocking modernization.

THE MIDDLE KINGDOM

When the merchant Marco Polo returned home to Venice from China at the end of the 13th century to report of a rich and powerful land superior to his own, few people believed him. How could a land remain virtually unknown and yet possess such wonders as paper currency, fireworks and combustible "black stones" (coal)?

But the stories were true. While Europeans were dragging themselves out of the Dark Ages, the Chinese were basking in a venerable civilization as sophisticated as any the world had ever known. So great were their achievements that as far back as the sixth century B.C. they had considered themselves a special people, living at the centre of the universe—the Middle Kingdom, as they called it.

For more than 2,000 years, their opinion of themselves was probably justified. But it was also dangerous, for it carried the seeds of their decline. Certain that they already had the best that was possible, they became obsessed with tradition and resisted most innovation from within or without. Feeling no need to traffic with inferior outsiders, early in their history the Chinese cut themselves off from foreign ideas and thus later found themselves defenceless when peoples of the West surpassed them in technology, commerce and military power.

Disdain for anything not Chinese was reinforced by the experience of invasion. Repeatedly, "barbarians" stormed out of the north or west to subjugate the country, instilling a justified dread of outsiders. But after every invasion, up to the 19th century, Chinese superiority eventually re-established itself. The invaders were simply assimilated—converted to Chinese ways so thoroughly that they became almost indistinguishable from the people who had lived there before them. For the Chinese, the result was two intertwined attitudes towards foreigners: they had to be feared, but their ideas and ways of life were not worth notice, much less emulation. Together, these two attitudes dominated Chinese thinking for millennia, and they help to explain much of the country's history.

At the time of Marco Polo's visit, that history had already assumed the peculiar cyclical pattern that has marked China's entire existence. Periods dominated by centralized regimes alternated with periods of anarchy, as powerful dynasties, each vying for control of the land and its people, rose to power, but were destroyed by internal dissension or foreign invasion.

Chinese history begins about 2200 B.C. with the Xia Dynasty, which ruled a kingdom centred in northern China, in the Yellow River valley. Little is known of it beyond myth, but it stimulated cultural growth that lasted more than 1,000 years, until about 770 B.C., when China fragmented into small feudal states, none strong enough to rule the others. This unsettled time continued for almost six centuries; yet despite political chaos, China gave promise of future cultural glory by producing two great philosopher-teachers. One was the wandering scholar Confucius; the other was a shadowy figure called Lao Zi, whose ideas became the basis for Daoism.

Both men sought to bring harmony to the brutal, disordered era in which they lived. But they chose very different ways. For Confucius, harmony was to be found in an ordered hierarchy of human relationships in which everyone accepted his place and behaved with virtue towards others. "Let the ruler be ruler," he said, "and the subject be subject."

For Lao Zi, harmony was achieved by withdrawing from worldly concerns and identifying instead with nature. He warned against attempts to interfere with the natural course of events, believing that interference was certain to be counterproductive. "Do nothing, and nothing will be not done," he counselled, suggesting that the universe proceeds smoothly according to rules that human beings cannot understand.

The ideas of both men coloured Chinese political thought for centuries. Confucian principles were used by later politicians to justify authoritarian government with strong centralized power. However, Confucianism burdened those in authority with responsibility for the welfare of their subjects. The do-nothing doctrine of Daoism also proved to be influential; it seems to explain, in the words of one observer, "the knack Chinese officials have for spontaneous inactivity", that is, for leaving well alone.

Although these philosophies were eventually to affect many facets of Chinese life, they did not do so immediately. They were paid little attention by

4

the feudal rulers in power at that time. Even when this troubled era ended in 221 B.C. with the unification of the Chinese people by the so-called First Emperor, the new leader accepted only part of Confucius' teaching—the part that called for obedience to authority. The requirement for authority to be humane—alert to the needs of its subjects—was disregarded by the First Emperor, an able but tyrannical ruler.

The First Emperor pulled together a fragmented people to make a nation governed by a strong, centralized government. The Great Wall was his creation, and he succeeded in attaching the name of his home state, Qin, to the whole country he had conquered.

Although the First Emperor had hoped that the empire he established would last "ten thousand generations", it outlived its founder by only four years. The regime that followed fared better, lasting from 206 B.C. to 220 A.D. It was founded by an upstart general, Liu Bang, who had been born a peasant. Liu commanded a ragtag army of renegade soldiers and bandits, which he placed at the service of a provincial warlord. In return he was given land—a sizeable kingdom he made into a power base from which he seized the imperial throne. He then gained favour with the population—nobility, gentry and peasantry alike—and consolidated his position by reducing taxes and relaxing the autocratic rule imposed by the First Emperor.

Liu Bang called his empire the Han, after the upper valley of the Han River, the region of his original kingdom, but its borders extended virtually to the limits of modern-day China—and its influence stretched almost to the furthest eastern reaches of the Roman Empire, on the shores of the Caspian Sea. The Han Empire was thus a power to reckon with throughout almost half the known world. Little wonder that even today Chinese refer to themselves as the Han, and that "Han characters" is the name given by the Japanese to Chinese writing.

The Han Dynasty improved the centralized government that had been introduced during the Qin Dynasty. Liu Bang, a peasant himself, was attuned to the needs and aspirations of common folk, and the ethical precepts of Confucianism eventually reasserted themselves. Thus the despotism of the Qin rulers gave way to a paternal benevolence that proved characteristic of many emperors.

Under Liu Bang and his successors, the emperor still ruled supreme, but he was advised by a council of ministers that was backed up, in turn, by a trained bureaucracy. Its members were selected on the basis of Confucian scholarship, not birth.

When the Han Dynasty fell, in the third century A.D., the country was once again plunged into a period of disorder. Indeed, the way in which the Han Dynasty degenerated is seen by Chinese scholars as a case study of the cyclical life of all dynasties.

According to their theories, a dynasty is always founded by a leader of great force and ability—in this case, Liu Bang. Surrounded by a close-knit band of capable advisers, and initially free of rivals, the leader devotes himself to the country's welfare, building walls, canals and roads, and maintaining order through systems of law and taxation that are administered fairly.

But the founder's successors are not always as capable and industrious as he. As the country prospers, the bureaucracy becomes inflated, and a luxury-loving court engages in factional in-fighting and intrigues. Taxes that formerly went into government coffers instead find their way into private hands, causing financial difficulties.

Sometimes a strong emperor can halt this downward trend. The Han Dynasty had such a man in Guang Wu Di, who ruled at the midpoint of its cycle and briefly checked its decline. But his successors were men of less ability, and the empire eventually broke into a multitude of small states ruled by local chieftains who were continually battling for supremacy.

The Han Dynasty lasted about 400 years and was followed by 400 years of anarchy. Strong, centralized government was re-established by the short-lived Sui Dynasty, which was followed by two exceptional dynasties, the Tang and Song. The Tang came first and lasted about 300 years. A brief period of trouble followed; then the Song gave China another three centuries of relative peace and prosperity, from 960 to 1279. The Tang and Song Dynasties formed the country's golden age.

Change and growth occurred in every aspect of Chinese life. In the arts (Chapter 3), great poetry, biographies and histories were written, and masterpieces of painting were created; potters sculpted intricately shaped porcelain vessels, decorating their surfaces with delicate carvings. In the realm of politics, frontiers expanded to include Korea and South-East Asia within China's orbit of influence. Government services improved, cities grew in size and sophistication, contact with the outside world increased, and science and technology advanced to the level that later astonished Marco Polo.

The bureaucracy, which had already proved its worth, was now refined into the final form that made it the model organization for civil administration. By the end of the Song period, it reputedly numbered more than 12,000 upper-level officials, selected for their intellectual qualities and understanding of the powerful moral principles of Confucianism.

In Han times, the members of this elite had been appointed on the recommendation of patrons who were held responsible for their honesty and efficiency; individual talent therefore counted for more than noble ancestry to the patrons making the appointments. Nonetheless, this patronage system eventually became corrupt; it was replaced in Sui times by a more egalitarian method, which was refined in Tang and Song times: entry and advancement came to be based on public examination, so that men of humble birth could rise to high position.

The examinations *(Chapter 3)* tested candidates for their fitness to serve in one of the nine ranks of the service, each of which had an upper and lower grade. To win entry to the highest levels, candidates were first tested on their knowledge of Chinese literature. This was followed by a second series of tests for judgment, writing ability, personal appearance and speaking ability, all designed to determine a candidate's aptitude for a specific post.

Students trained for these examinations in schools in the various provinces and, for more advanced study, went to the capital city. Everywhere, the curriculum was based on Confucian ideology—which automatically assured the government of consistency and helped to unify the country.

The broader opportunities afforded to men by the civil service examinations were just one aspect of the social

Tai Zu, the Emperor who founded the Song Dynasty in 960, looks the grim tyrant in this portrait. Actually he was a patron of the arts, a wily and generous politician who bought off enemies, and a reformer of the bureaucracy. His reign occurred in the midst of six centuries of peaceful achievement in culture and commerce.

A BRILLIANT YET TORMENTED HISTORY

400,000 B.C. The Yellow River valley is occupied by bands of *Homo erectus*, the evolutionary forerunners of *Homo sapiens*. Like others of their kind in Europe, Africa and South-East Asia, these early humans use fire and shape tools from stone.

4500–2500 B.C. In Gansu province in the North, a Neolithic farming culture, one of many at this time, produces fine painted pottery *(above)*.

c. 2200–1766 B.C. According to Chinese histories, a dynasty called the Xia flourishes; its people domesticate animals, grow wheat and make silk.

1766–1122 B.C. Inscriptions on more than 100,000 tortoise shells and bones describe events and customs during the Shang Dynasty, the first with a verifiable history. During the Shang era the Chinese perfect the wheel, employ chariots in warfare, carve jade and ivory and make vessels of bronze.

1122–221 B.C. The Zhou Dynasty: early Emperors extend the rule of the government to the Yangtze valley, but the dynasty's power dwindles after 771 B.C., as local warlords defy the Emperors and battle with each other. Iron casting is invented *(below)*, as are the multiplication tables.

600–300 B.C. Great philosopher-teachers appear as the Zhou Dynasty declines: Lao Zi (sixth century B.C.), Confucius (551–479 B.C.) and Mencius (372–289 B.C.).

221–206 B.C. The vigorous but short-lived Qin Dynasty is founded by a warrior king called Shi Huang Di, who builds the Great Wall as well as canals, roads and palaces. During his reign, a uniform writing system and standardized weights and measures

come into use. But Shi Huang Di orders the burning of books *(above)* considered subversive to his rule.

202 B.C.–220 A.D. Peasant-born Liu Bang founds the Han Dynasty. One of his great successors, Wu Di, who reigns from 141 to 87 B.C., conquers southern China, northern Vietnam and part of Korea, and forges trade routes through Central Asia to India and Persia. Under the Han rulers, science and technology make remarkable strides: paper, the compass and the seismograph are invented, sunspots studied, and steel manufactured. The first census is taken. China's population in 2 A.D.: 57,671,400.

220–589 After the collapse of the Han Dynasty, China once more splits into warring kingdoms. The long period of instability is known as that of the Three Kingdoms and the Northern and Southern Dynasties.

589–618 The Sui Dynasty Emperors, Wen Di and Yang Di, reunite the country after four centuries of chaos. They build a great transportation network, including the Grand Canal, exhausting the treasury and the people.

618–907 A Sui official, Li Yuan, founds the Tang Dynasty. Early Tang Emperors expand their control deep into Asia; in the seventh century, China rules from Korea to Iran, from the Mongolian border to Vietnam. The later and more peaceful Tang period fosters a golden age of learning and the arts. The great Chinese poets Li Bai and Du Fu flourish, as do the painters Wu Daozi and Wang Wei. Fine silks and lacquer ware are manufactured; music and dance thrive.

960–1279 After the Tang Dynasty collapses into a half century of internecine warfare, the Song Dynasty restores power and momentum to Chinese society. The inventions of movable type and paper money, accompanied by another remarkable flowering of art and literature, mark a zenith of Chinese culture. The Song government retreats to the southern part of China when barbarians from the North, the Jürchen, conquer northern China and found the Jin Dynasty there in 1126.

1215–1368 Genghis Khan, leading horsemen like the one below, sacks Peking in 1215. The Mongols conquer the Jin Empire in 1234 and a year later invade the Song refuge in southern China. In 1271 Genghis' grandson Kublai Khan founds the Yuan Dynasty and establishes the elaborate court described by Marco Polo.

1368–1644 A peasant-born Buddhist novice named Zhu Yuanzhang unites rebel groups, overturns the Yuan and begins the Ming Dynasty. Known for its superb porcelain, a Chinese invention, the Ming era is also one of important deeds. Ming Emperors build the Imperial Palace in Peking, reconstruct and extend the Great Wall *(opposite, above)*, and dispatch sea-going junks *(opposite, centre)* that explore South-East Asia and reach the Red Sea.

1644–1839 The Manchu invade from the North and set up the last imperial

dynasty, the Qing. During the reign of Emperor Kang Xi (1661–1722), Chinese influence is extended to Mongolia, Central Asia, Tibet, Korea, Annam, Burma and Thailand. But by the 19th century, blind adherence to obsolete ways, corruption within and a new enemy without—European traders and their opium *(below)*—undermine Manchu rule.

1839–1911 A series of wars and rebellions, all humiliating defeats to China, increases foreign domination. Imperial efforts to halt opium imports ignite the First Opium War

(1839–1842), which forces the cession of Hong Kong to the British, and the opening of Shanghai and other ports to

foreign trade. The Second Opium War (1856–1860), involving both the British and the French, is followed by disastrous wars first with France (1884–1885) and later with Japan (1894–1895). Anger over such defeats finds vent in the catastrophic Taiping Rebellion (1850–1864), which is suppressed with some help from

Europeans, and the Boxer Rebellion (1900–1901), in which foreign troops *(below, left)* intervene; their governments then demand additional territorial concessions and huge indemnities. In spite of these losses, the Empress Dowager Ci Xi (1835–1908)—a concubine who seized power by imprisoning her nephew, the Emperor—rules with ruinously misdirected rigidity, crushing several attempts to modernize the country.

1911–1925 Revolutionary groups, inspired by Dr. Sun Yat-sen, a Western-educated physician, succeed in overthrowing the Qing in 1911, bringing to an end more than 2,000 years of intermittent imperial rule by eight major dynasties. His political party, the Kuomintang (KMT), which after World War I includes Soviet-backed Communists, attempts to unite the country, but is able to control only parts of the South. Much of the rest of China is ruled by corrupt and brutal local warlords.

1925–1931 After the death of Sun Yat-sen in 1925, Chiang Kai-shek *(below)* takes control of the KMT and wins China from the warlords. At first allied with the Communists, he splits with them to seek full control. In 1927, Communist activists, including one of the party's most influential thinkers, Chou En-lai, lead Shanghai workers in taking over parts of the city. To check the Communists' increasing power, KMT troops massacre thousands of people in Shanghai.

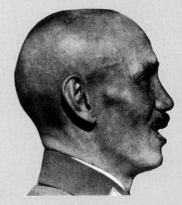

1931–1933 Japanese expand their foothold in Manchuria, Chinese territory they had won in 1905; they occupy areas in the north-east that were controlled by China.

1934–1935 In the epic Long March, Communists, driven from their south-eastern bases in Jiangxi and Hunan by

Chiang Kai-shek's "extermination campaigns", set off for remote Shaanxi province. Some 100,000 begin the 9,500-kilometre trek; about 8,000 survive to regroup and retrain in caves in Shaanxi. Mao Tse-tung emerges as the Communist leader.

1937 Japanese armies in Manchuria *(below)* flood into China, quickly seizing Peking, Shanghai and Nanjing. The following year China's government is forced to take refuge in remote Chongqing in Sichuan province.

1941–1945 In World War II, the United States and Soviet Union supply Chiang's forces—the Nationalists—with armies to fight the Japanese. No foreign aid goes directly to Mao's Communists, but they raise and arm troops and fight the Japanese more vigorously than the Nationalists do.

1945–1947 After the defeat of Japan, a U.S. mission led by General George C. Marshall tries to form a coalition government, bringing together Mao's Communists and the Nationalists. The attempt fails, however, and the civil war intensifies. At first the Nationalists

gain the advantage, forcing Mao to abandon the Communist stronghold in Yan'an *(below, left)*.

1949 Communists crush Chiang's forces and take control of mainland China, establishing the People's

Republic of China, with its capital in Peking. Chiang and the remnants of the Kuomintang carry their flag *(above)* to the island of Taiwan and set up the Nationalist regime there.

1950 All land is seized from private owners and redistributed. The regime's opponents—real or suspected—are executed or sent to labour camps.

1953 Mao initiates the first Five-Year Plan for the industrialization of China.

1955—1957 Collectivization of agriculture begins with organization of farmers into co-operatives. Mao's regime invites criticism in the Hundred Flowers campaign; critics are later punished.

1958 Farmers are organized into communes. Mao institutes the Great Leap Forward, a misguided scheme designed to hasten industrial and agricultural production through decentralization. The programme is a disaster, disrupting the economy and helping to bring on famine.

1960 The Soviet Union withdraws technical advisers and stops economic aid to China—the onset of open antagonism between the two largest Communist nations.

1966 The Great Proletarian Cultural Revolution begins as a million young Red Guard activists parade in Peking. Mao calls for "continuous revolution" and accuses a number of more moderate colleagues, including Liu Shaoqi and Deng Xiaoping, of trying to reinstitute capitalism. Mao's wife, Jiang Qing, appointed dictator of Chinese culture, suppresses "liberal" and Western influences in art and

literature. China enters a period of social and political anarchy.

1971 The People's Republic of China is admitted to the United Nations, obtaining the seat on the Security Council formerly held by Chiang's Taiwan-based Nationalist government.

1972 The excesses of the Cultural Revolution subside; many people banished for political sins return to influence. U.S. President Nixon visits China, marking the great change in relations between the two countries.

1976 Both the old leaders, Chou En-lai *(below)* and Mao Tse-tung, die. Four radical party members, led by Mao's widow, attempt to assume power but are outmanoeuvred by the moderates, who arrest the "Gang of Four".

1981 The Chinese leadership, headed by pragmatists such as Deng Xiaoping, officially declares the Cultural Revolution a catastrophe and moves towards more liberal economic policies.

1988-1989 Inflation tops 20 per cent. A campaign is launched against official

corruption. In Tibet, demonstrations for self-determination are bloodily suppressed. China and the Soviet Union formally end their 30-year estrangement. Units of the PLA open fire on students occupying Tiananmen Square in protest at the government's refusal to grant greater political freedoms. After a violent clampdown on dissenters, martial law is lifted in 1990. The government stresses its commitment to communist orthodoxy.

changes that accompanied the prosperity of the times. Landlords and gentry moved into town and showed more inclination to amuse themselves with theatres, restaurants, and wine and tea shops than with the country pleasures of hunting and horseback riding. But along with this growing sophistication, there were other less felicitous developments. The status of women declined. More and more they were confined to their homes ("a virtuous woman," it was said, "never takes three steps beyond the threshold"). Men had concubines and, around the year 950, the curious custom arose of binding women's feet to keep them small and dainty, apparently in imitation of the tiny feet of a dancer admired then by the imperial court.

Foot-binding normally began when a girl was five and continued for several years until the feet stopped growing. The intense pain of this deliberate mutilation has been described by a modern-day victim: "My feet hurt so much that for two years I had to walk on my hands and knees. Sometimes at night they hurt so much I could not sleep. I stuck my feet under my mother and she lay on them so they hurt less."

By the time the binding was finished the feet were very small indeed: "Two fingers could be inserted in the cleft between the front of the foot and the heel." So sought-after was this trait that marriage brokers were commonly asked about the size of a girl's feet rather than the beauty of her face. Indeed, big feet were considered so unfeminine that foot-binding continued even after it was officially banned at the beginning of the 20th century.

A third momentous change helps to explain why cities became increasingly important during China's golden age.

Industry and commerce were booming. China now welcomed foreign trade, and though commerce was considered demeaning, it was very profitable and contributed to the growth of a large merchant class. The trade was carried out by Chinese ships calling at ports on the Indian Ocean and by caravans of Arabs, Indians and Persians—and a few intrepid Europeans—that made their way overland via the old Silk Road: vast expanses of desert and mountain trails winding from Antioch on the Mediterranean coast to Samarkand and Kashgar, and into Chang'an in central China.

Silk and porcelain were the articles coveted by the rest of the world; at the time neither was made in the West. During the Tang and Song Dynasties the Chinese were so advanced technologically that some historians believe the country stood at the threshold of an industrial revolution. According to Joseph Needham, the Cambridge University authority on this subject, the Chinese were ahead of Europeans in developing the wheelbarrow by 10 centuries, the crossbow by 13 centuries, draught-animal harnesses by eight centuries, cast iron by 12 centuries, porcelain by 13 centuries and mechanical clocks by six centuries.

They built sophisticated astronomical instruments to track the movements of the moon and stars in 130 A.D. During the first century, holes about 600 metres deep were drilled to tap underground salt resources. Gunpowder was first put to use in the ninth century, for firework displays; by the 12th century it was being used in military grenades and rockets. Like gunpowder, the compass, invented around the first century A.D., had an origin unrelated to utilitarian concerns. It was

first employed to indicate an auspicious orientation for grave sites and was not adapted to ocean navigation until the 11th century.

Yet practical needs prompted other Chinese inventions. As long ago as 800 B.C., foundry workers began to mass produce iron axe blades, plough tips, belt buckles and axle fittings by the stack-casting method, which still serves today for precision parts such as gears. An ancient foundry excavated at Wenxian, in Henan province, in the 1970s contained 500 sets of multiple moulds, some still usable. The moulds came in 16 different designs in 36 sizes and could turn out as many as 84 identical units per mould. Such mass production of superior parts for farming equipment resulted in a dramatic increase in food production—and therefore in the size of the population.

Perhaps the most significant of all Chinese developments was the printing of books, which stimulated literacy at a time when in Europe even many kings could not read or write. Printing required three separate inventions: paper, ink and type. Paper came first; its invention is attributed to Cai Lun, a eunuch who in 105 A.D. was *shang fang ling*, the Emperor's director of the manufacture of furniture and weapons. According to a biography written a few centuries later, "Cai Lun thought of using tree bark, hemp, rags and fishnets" to replace bamboo and silk cloth as writing surfaces. He "received high praise for his ability," but later was caught up in disastrous intrigues between the Empress and the Emperor's grandmother, and "he went home, took a bath, combed his hair, put on his best robes and drank poison."

No such fate is recorded for the other key inventors. Chinese ink—a mixture

Kublai Khan *(centre, in ermine)*, who
in the year 1260 completed the
Mongol conquest of China started by
his grandfather Genghis, crosses a
desert with his retinue. A camel
caravan passes in the background.

of lampblack and gum, moulded into sticks—was devised by Wei Dan early in the third century. By the eighth century, ink and paper were being used for wood-block printing, but books did not become common until later. According to a valuable account, "In the year 931 the Prime Minister Feng Dao, together with Li Yu, petitioned the Emperor" to order the printing of the Confucian classics. "Following this the use of printed literature became general throughout the empire."

Chinese printing was almost always done from blocks of wood—jujube or pear—the size of two book pages. The pages were first handwritten on a sheet of translucent paper so that the characters' ink could be transferred to the wood surface. Next a skilled cutter carved around the transferred characters to make them stand out in relief. Ink was applied to the block, then a blank sheet was laid on and brushed lightly to pick up the print. There were no presses, but this method enabled a single worker to turn out several thousand printed pages in a day.

The Chinese also invented movable type—the invention credited by a contemporary writer to "Bi Sheng, a man of the common people"—in about 1050, four centuries before Johann Gutenberg reinvented it in Germany, but they never made much use of it. Their non-phonetic writing, which at that time contained some 30,000 different characters, made typesetting quite impractical; until the 20th century, Chinese printers found it easier to hand-cut an entire two-page block of characters than to assemble the pages from separate cast-type characters that had to be laboriously selected from hundreds of bins and trays.

It was China at its peak that Marco Polo observed when he arrived there in 1275. The Song Dynasty of southern China by then had been replaced by the Yuan. This dynasty was the first to be established by a Mongol invader; the founder was Kublai Khan, the grandson of the dreaded Genghis Khan, whose hordes of hard-riding, fur-clad horsemen had swept over much of Asia and eastern Europe.

The Mongols were one of the barbarian peoples feared and detested by the Chinese. "They smell so bad one cannot approach them," wrote a chronicler. But like the invaders who had preceded and those who followed them, the Mongols—including Kublai Khan himself—eventually adopted Chinese ways and accepted elements of Chinese culture. The government bureaucracy remained intact, and the traditional Chinese regard for artistic and intellectual achievement endured.

By this time, however, the great outpouring of Tang and Song innovation, creativity and growth had reached its zenith. Chinese culture did not disintegrate; it simply coasted along for some six centuries at a more or less even level, punctuated by occasional outbursts of achievement.

One of the most remarkable of these spurts of activity was the far-ranging maritime exploration that took place during the dynasty that followed the Yuan: the Ming. Navigating by compass, no fewer than seven expeditions sailed the southern seas in huge junks, some more than 100 metres long, with four decks and watertight compartments. Over a period of 28 years, beginning in 1405, their voyages took them first to South-East Asia and India, then successively to Hormuz on the Persian Gulf, to East Africa, to the Gulf of Aden at the mouth of the Red

Sea, and up the Red Sea as far as Jidda, the port city for Mecca.

The admiral who carried out the voyages was a eunuch named Zheng He, who served in the Ming court. Of Mongol descent, Zheng had been captured by Chinese forces at the age of 10 and had been castrated. Attached to the army as an orderly, he rose rapidly, eventually attracting the attention of the imperial court.

For centuries, the Chinese Emperors had used eunuchs as court functionaries and guards for the imperial harem, positions in which they were naturally privy to the inner workings of court politics. Many were consulted now and then on policy matters, and many, like the ill-fated inventor of paper, reached high rank outside the harem. Such a person was Zheng He.

Zheng was little more than 30 years old when the Emperor selected him to command a series of maritime expeditions designed to bring tribute to the Middle Kingdom. Whatever the new admiral's qualifications, they must have included considerable administrative ability, for his first fleet consisted of no fewer than 62 ships and a force of 28,000 men. At each stop he was to make known the Emperor's desire for tribute; "if they refused to submit," according to the official account, "force was used to coerce them."

From his seven voyages, Zheng brought tribute-bearing delegations from 36 countries. These emissaries presented the Emperor with such gifts as ostriches, zebras and giraffes. Then, after 1433, the expeditions ceased as suddenly as they had been inaugurated. Apparently, the Confucian bureaucrats disapproved of the voyages as a wasteful frivolity. China no longer showed any interest

in becoming a maritime power, thus leaving the way open for other seafarers—the Portuguese, the Dutch, the British, the Japanese and the Americans—to control the waters surrounding China and, eventually, to prey on China itself.

The last imperial dynasty to rule China, the Qing, was founded by Manchu invaders from the north-east who overthrew the Ming in 1644. Once again the outsiders became assimilated, bequeathing to Chinese culture only one relic of Manchu tradition: the custom of wearing hair in a braided queue. Ordained by the Manchus in order to remove all external vestiges of Ming rule, the hairstyle was so harshly enforced throughout the empire that Westerners, visiting China generations later and seeing pigtails everywhere, assumed that it was a purely and typically Chinese style.

Under the Manchus, a long stretch of peace and prosperity lulled China into thinking that all was well. But the rapid development of Western civilization had by then made the Middle Kingdom a backwater, its traditional economy and social organization anachronisms. The first waves of Western intervention, which was ultimately to destroy the fabric of Chinese life, were already cresting on the horizon.

Among the earliest Westerners to enter China were missionaries, who arrived in the 13th century. More significant in the long run were the merchants who followed. Few found a warm welcome. A group of Portuguese who arrived in Canton in 1517 were ordered to be held for three days in a temple to learn proper manners. Only then were they permitted to travel to Peking for an audience with the Emperor—where their days of training

In a 19th-century opium den, four men share pipes of the narcotic, inhaling vapours from a small heated ball in the pipe bowl. Expenditures on opium brought into China by Western dealers so drained the economy that the government tried to suppress the drug. The result was the Opium Wars, a series of clashes with Britain and France between 1839 and 1860.

Chinese victims of the Opium Wars lie inside their ruined fort at Taku, in northern China, after a battle that pitted crossbows (one is visible on top of the wall) against British and French muskets. Western victories assured foreign domination of China for almost a century.

came to naught. Annoyed by their "lack of respect", the Emperor expelled them from the country.

But the money to be made from China's valued silks, porcelain and tea was too tempting. As pressure from Western merchants mounted, the government sought to control foreign trade by ruling, in 1757, that henceforth all of it should move only through the port of Canton, controlled by a dozen merchant associations, or hongs, appointed by the government to deal exclusively with foreigners.

Chafing under these restrictions, the Europeans—especially the British, who dominated the China trade in the 18th century—petitioned the Emperor for treaties extending their rights. They got nowhere. One British mission was turned away because the very idea of trading with another nation as equals was alien to the rulers of the Middle Kingdom. A second, under Lord Amherst, was summarily shown the door when Amherst refused to kowtow to the Emperor.

This gesture of respect—a ceremonial succession of three bows, each followed by a prostration, with the nose touching the floor—was routinely used by all Chinese on meeting people of higher rank. Children kowtowed to their parents and courtiers kowtowed to the Emperor; and the Emperor kowtowed to heaven. Amherst, however, considered the practice to be demeaning, and the Chinese viewed his refusal to follow the customs of the country as simply one more example of barbarian bad manners.

Into this stalemate in the early days of the 19th century was introduced another element: opium. It was probably first brought into the country as a narcotic, mixed with tobacco, by Dutch traders during the 17th century (the Dutch at that time were smoking

the mixture in their own colonies in Java and Taiwan).

In 1729, when the Chinese opium traffic was still quite small—200 chests a year—the Emperor banned it. But the restriction was widely ignored. By 1790, more than 4,000 chests were being imported from India alone, and by the late 1830s, just before the Opium War, the annual flow had reached a staggering 30,000 chests.

For the avaricious merchants— British, Portuguese, American and French—who engaged in it, the opium trade was a market that could never dry up. A customer, once gained, could never be lost. Addiction to opium, according to one Chinese report, had spread from the gentry, the people who could afford it, to "artisans, merchants, women and even Buddhist monks and Daoist priests".

So great was the traffic, that China's trade balance was affected. More money was now leaving the country than entering it. "If the opium trade is not stopped," reported the Imperial Commissioner at Canton, "the country will become poorer and poorer and its people weaker and weaker. Eventually not only will there be inadequate funds to support an army, there will be no useful soldiers at all."

In 1838, the Emperor ordered the Imperial Commissioner of Canton to eliminate the opium traffic. The commissioner in turn demanded that all foreign traders surrender the opium they had on hand. They complied, and in 1839 the commissioner had all 20,000 chests burnt in public. Then he asked the traders to stop bringing opium into China, but the British indignantly refused. Tensions mounted, and a minor fracas involving British

4

seamen became the tinder that ignited the First Opium War.

It was a one-sided contest. The Chinese were unprepared to fight and really did not want to. They wanted only to stop the opium traffic, which they considered immoral. The British seized several cities along the coast. When they threatened to move up the Yangtze River to Nanjing, the Chinese sued for peace.

In the resulting treaty, China ceded Hong Kong to Britain and agreed to pay the conquerors 21 million Mexican dollars in indemnity; it also agreed to open four ports besides Canton to foreign trade, and to exempt foreigners living in them from Chinese law. There was no mention of curtailing the opium trade that had started the War.

The Qing rulers, stunned by the defeat and the terms of the treaty, faltered. The British, taking advantage of China's vulnerability, struck again, this time aided by the French. Once more the Chinese were routed, and once more treaties were signed, opening more ports and giving foreigners additional rights.

This fresh insult helped to fuel a massive populist uprising in 1850. It was led by a Cantonese mystic named Hong Xiuchuan, a convert to Christianity who believed that he was Jesus Christ's younger brother. Hong recruited followers from among poor peasants by demanding sweeping reforms, including equality for women, the abolition of private property and the distribution of surplus harvest to areas suffering from famine.

Hong called his movement *taiping tianguo*, which means "Heavenly Kingdom of Great Peace", and his Taiping Rebellion was initially a success. Although they were ill-trained and ill-

THE LONG MARCH

Survivors of the Long March trained to fight again in Yan'an, a city of caves in Shaanxi.

Few ordeals in history rival the 9,500-kilometre hegira that the Chinese proudly remember as *chang zheng*, the "Long March". It was a flight of Communist forces from almost certain defeat by the Nationalists; yet from this retreat emerged the essential ingredients of Communist triumph.

In October of 1934, the Nationalist Army was poised to crush the Red Army enclave in south central Jiangxi province. Some 100,000 men—and 35 women—burst through the encircling forces and began a fighting retreat. The straggling columns fought off pursuing Nationalists, then bandits and hostile tribes of Hsi-Fan and Mantzu (the Mantzu queen threatened to boil alive anyone who helped the retreating army). "There were so very many battles," recalled one survivor, "that when I look back, it seems to be one enormous battle going on forever."

The natural enemies were worse: heat and hunger, thirst and cold, mountains, rivers and swampland into which the unwary quickly sank out of sight. More than a year after the march began, the Communists finally found refuge in Yan'an, a remote mountain outpost in the shadow of the Great Wall. Fewer than 8,000 people had survived— an adversity-hardened nucleus of leaders for the military and social upheaval that was still to come.

equipped, Hong's peasant soldiers routed the antiquated Imperial Army and moved north, seizing city after city. When they reached Nanjing, they made it their capital, and they held it for 11 years. Curiously, the structure of the Taiping regime was much like that of modern China: "We shall till together and enjoy the fruits of our labour in common," it proclaimed. The basic social unit was a collective made up of 25 "comrade" households; schooling was mandatory for everyone, and women served as functionaries on a par with men—there were even women in the Taiping army.

Ironically, the Taiping regime was brought down not by the Imperial Army, which was completely ineffectual, but by two provincial militias financed in part by Western interests; the Westerners assumed a Qing government would be easier to deal with than the Taiping regime. In the summer of 1864, one of these provincial armies reached Nanjing. Hong Xiuchuan, seeing the handwriting on the wall, committed suicide. A month later the city fell. "Not a single man of the 100,000 bandits in the city responded to the order to surrender," reported one of the army's leaders. "They burnt themselves alive in groups as if they had no regrets."

Handed this reprieve, the Qing regime made a few feeble attempts at reform, one of them undertaken in 1898 by the youthful Emperor Guang Xu. But Guang Xu's ageing aunt Ci Xi, Empress Dowager and a former concubine, disapproved. Staging what amounted to a *coup d'état*, she seized power from her nephew and had him thrown into prison.

Then, in a final fiasco for the Qing Dynasty, Empress Ci Xi backed an uprising by a semi-religious group known as the Society of the Righteous and Harmonious Fists, whose aim was to drive all foreigners from Chinese soil. Commonly known as the Boxers because of their ritualistic shadowboxing, members of the group believed themselves to be immune to Western bullets. With the Empress Ci Xi's permission, the Boxers attacked all the foreign legations in Peking—with predictable results. Thousands of foreign troops, among them Russians, Japanese, Americans, British and French, came to the rescue. The Empress Dowager regained power briefly, but the Qing Dynasty was, to all intents and purposes, over.

The last dynasty was finally replaced in 1912 by a republic, China's first. The new government was founded by Sun Yat-sen, a former medical doctor, who had worked for years to make China a democracy. However, for the next 37 years, no single person or group was able to control the country for long. For most of that time, parts of China were ruled by one or another provincial warlord intent on getting his hands on tax revenues.

Sun Yat-sen's Nationalist Party, the Kuomintang (KMT), lost power a month after toppling the Empire. The party disbanded, eventually to be reestablished after the end of World War I. At that time Marxism also gained popularity among Chinese intellectuals, and Marxist leaders became prominent in the top levels of the KMT. In 1921, the Chinese Communist Party was founded, with help from Russian Bolsheviks, at a Congress in Shanghai. (Mao Tse-tung was the delegate from Hunan.) For a few years the CCP and the KMT collaborated fitfully and warily in trying to win the country, first from the warlords—and later from each other.

In 1927 an alliance of Communist and Nationalist forces, led by Sun Yat-sen's successor, a young military officer named Chiang Kai-shek, gained control from the warlords. Soon afterwards, however, Chiang attacked the Communists, and for the next 22 years the two rival revolutionary forces fought to rule China. They united again briefly during World War II, to fight uneasily together against a common enemy, Japan, which invaded China in 1937. But at the end of the global conflict, with Japan gone from the scene, Nationalists and Communists again turned on each other, plunging the Middle Kingdom into civil war. In 1948 the Communists under the leadership of Mao Tse-tung destroyed Chiang's army in two decisive operations, one in Manchuria and the other in the Huai River basin in north central China. By 1949, Chiang and his Nationalist government had fled to refuge on Taiwan, a nearby island that at various times over the centuries was controlled by the Dutch, Japanese and Chinese. On October 1, 1949, Mao Tse-tung proclaimed a unified nation as a Communist state, the People's Republic of China.

ORDEAL OF THE CIVIL WAR

The clink of glasses raised by Mao Tse-tung and Chiang Kai-shek *(below)* in 1945 echoed a false harmony. For two decades these implacable rivals had competed for control of China, their struggle interrupted only by the need for joint resistance against invasion by Japan—and by the intervention of the United States, which envisioned a China ruled by coalition as the bulwark of post-war Asia.

Coalition was impossible. Already bleeding from years of Japanese aggression, China was plunged into four terrible years of civil war. Chiang's Nationalist party controlled most of the cities, and his three million troops boasted superior arms. But Mao's Communists found succour in agrarian China, where impoverished, exploited peasants were ready for a new order. Simultaneously, disgruntled wage earners and intellectuals became so disillusioned by government corruption and economic chaos that they abandoned the Nationalists. The Communist guerrillas, outnumbered 3 to 1 at first, quickly won recruits and, after a few victories, a flood of defections from the Nationalists. At one point an entire division of 8,000 men changed sides. By 1949, the cities, too, were Mao's. Chiang and two million loyalists fled to Taiwan, leaving behind towns in ruins, a collapsed economy and a population in danger of starvation.

Momentarily at peace, Mao Tse-tung and Chiang Kai-shek share a toast in Chongqing in 1945.

Racked with grief, a peasant wails her suffering amid the rubble of the Civil War, which cost 11 to 12 million lives and left millions more destitute.

Fleeing the battle zone, Chinese civilians carrying their remaining food and possessions swarm down from a train that has brought them to the Nationalist-held Yangtze River town of Pukou near Nanjing.

Their currency almost worthless
from inflation, desperate citizens of
Shanghai press to enter a bank that
was exchanging paper money for
gold. Seven people died in the crush.

A 12-year-old pressed into Nationalist uniform as an infantry helper kneels to drink from a fellow soldier's canteen before shipping out to the battle of Huai Hai in late 1948. The Nationalists lost half a million men there.

An old woman uses a twig broom to sweep up kernels of precious rice spilled on a railway platform in 1948. By then, most farmland was in Communist hands and available food went mainly to the military, leaving Nationalist-held cities desperately short of essential supplies.

The Communist victory won, lorryloads of troops roll through Peking, traditional capi

China, on January 31, 1949. Most of the lorries in the triumphal parade were American-made, captured from the Nationalists.

A man bows before a black-draped portrait of Mao Tse-tung in Peking's Tiananmen Square. Mao died in 1976, bringing an end to the period of internal convulsion known as the Cultural Revolution.

RED GUARD AND OLD GUARD

In 1966, a six-year-old girl named Lihua was banished from Peking with all her family to her father's ancestral village of Gold Mountain, 1,300 kilometres to the south. Her father was a respected science teacher in a Peking school, but in his youth he had served briefly in the armies of the anti-Communist Kuomintang. That was enough, in the political frenzy of 1966, to warrant denunciation and punishment.

Before escorting the family to the train that would take them into exile, youthful radicals ransacked their flat, confiscated the mother's jewellery and built a bonfire of their books, furniture and photographs. When Lihua and her family arrived in Gold Mountain, local officials relieved them of the rest of their belongings, leaving them only the clothing on their bodies. They were then shunted into an abandoned schoolhouse, its windows gone, its roof leaky.

In the days that followed, Lihua's parents were repeatedly paraded through the village streets. Her father, wearing round his neck a placard proclaiming him to be a hidden counter-revolutionary was urged to confess his supposed crimes in public. Both father and mother were beaten with iron bars. Within a month Lihua's mother was dead and her father was deaf and permanently crippled.

The six-year-old Lihua became a rice-winner, helping her brothers support the family by trudging into the hills to chop firewood, which she sold to the operators of a village brick kiln. Lacking both experience and muscle, she sometimes cut herself with the axe; the wounds never healed properly because, as a member of the criminal class, Lihua was not eligible for the village's medical programme. She begged, sold eggs and husked rice. She prowled the woods for mushrooms and edible roots, now and again making herself sick with her mistakes.

Despite her wounds, chronic hunger and illness, Lihua managed to survive one of the most violent political convulsions in human history—Mao Tse-tung's Great Proletarian Cultural Revolution. This upheaval began in 1966 and moderated in 1969, but did not clearly come to an end for a decade. By then, it had ruined the lives of 100 million Chinese people.

The cataclysm was clearly the work of Chairman Mao, but it was not simply the result of some aberration in the mind of an ageing leader. It grew also out of Chinese history, and it was prompted by pressures from the outside world. Most important, the Cultural Revolution as well as other upheavals which have convulsed the People's Republic before and since were the products of inherent strains within the Chinese Communist Party (CCP) itself. These tensions sprang from opposing concepts of the best methods for building a new society out of the ruins of the old.

The CCP leadership has consistently tried to present an outward picture of perfect Marxist unanimity. Within, it has often been riven from top to bottom by factions on the left and right. The members on the left, often called radicals, have believed passionately that the road to a socialist society should be travelled without deviation, and quickly. They have wanted to discard all practices of the past and to establish a wholly new order. The aim has been absolute equality, a pure socialism that grants everybody the same share of opportunity, of work and of reward without regard to either ability or individual contribution.

Those members to the right, also sincere revolutionaries, have believed just as passionately in proceeding with care, testing each step for its pragmatic worth, and perhaps even retaining some elements of the past. They have been old-fashioned enough to believe that reward should be commensurate with merit and achievement, and they have even believed it wise to preserve some remnants of private enterprise side by side with state ownership. To the leftist radicals, these backsliders—stigmatized as "capitalist roaders, running dogs, radish reds"—have been anathema.

Such deep and bitter antagonisms have caused great tension within China's ruling circle. When the interior stresses have broken to the surface they have brought bewildering gyrations of policy, and social and economic chaos. In the 1960s they drove the nation to the edge of civil war.

It was never easy to determine precisely where Chairman Mao stood among the contending elements. While he was the initiator, on record at least, of the abrupt swings in policy that repeatedly threw the country into confusion, he was likewise the first to back away when the swing went too far and matters skidded out of control.

For the most part, Mao's heart was with the left, in that he longed for some absolutely pure, new social order, untainted by the past. Counterbalancing Mao was his comrade in decades of military and political battle, Chou En-lai; Chou appeared to be the stabilizing influence, the veteran who held things together when the parts threatened to fly off in every direction.

When Mao, Chou and the CCP first won control in the 1949 Liberation, they found little to work with; there was no room at first for dissension. After 28 years of war capped by a political death struggle, the nation was a shambles. It was bankrupt and swamped by inflation, the industrial base in ruins and the transportation network crippled.

About the only asset at hand in abundance was people—if anything, an overabundance. But many were eager, after centuries of deprivation, for the changes promised by the CCP. With this support, Mao and the CCP set out to create a modern Communist state with the economic, social and military sinews to stand as an equal among the world's great powers.

Between 1950 and 1956, Mao and the party appeared to be succeeding. They nationalized industry and commerce. They stabilized the economy and brought the nation's finances under control. By brutal force they redistributed farmland, destroying in the process the rural gentry who for centuries had ruled the lives of landless peasants. According to one estimate, two million landowners were murdered. The survivors and their descendants were stigmatized as coming

from a "bad class background", a label that made advancement virtually impossible in modern China.

Life was transformed. Prostitution, drug use and bribery, once endemic, were to a great extent eliminated. Women were released from their status as chattel, concubinage was outlawed; nearly all the children were sent to school; and practically all able adults—male and female—were put to work in fields, factories or offices.

At first the CCP accepted Soviet guidance in "building socialism", but later they came to doubt, then detest the Russian connection. This growing distrust may have helped precipitate two social upheavals that preceded the Cultural Revolution itself. More specifically, they seem to have been reactions to crises that shook the U.S.S.R. in 1956: in February, Soviet leader Nikita Khrushchev gave a speech violently attacking Joseph Stalin; in October, Hungarians revolted against Soviet domination. It seemed that not even a dead deity of Communism was safe from his successors and, worse, that there were flaws in Communist rule severe enough to provoke unarmed subjects to resist their masters by throwing rocks at tanks.

Mao, a living deity aware of the lurking schisms among his own top leaders, appears to have been particularly perturbed by these danger signals from abroad. He decided to invite his people more deeply into the embrace of the party, even asking them to speak up to suggest improvements to the system. In the spring of 1956, Mao launched the Hundred Flowers Campaign, so named because, with that uniquely Chinese flair for poetic metaphor in political rhetoric, he urged that the workers and peasants "let a hundred flowers bloom and let a hundred schools of thought contend".

He got more than he had bargained for. Soon China's leaders were reeling before a storm of criticism—from writers and intellectuals, from would-be political activists, from people inside and outside the party. When some went so far as to advocate the establishment of a multilateral system, Mao did an about-face and decreed that the hundred flowers should forthwith wilt.

Many paid dearly for their temerity. Some were jailed, others lost their jobs and became political outcasts. One CCP official, a school administrator who had criticized the arrogance of fellow party functionaries, found himself violently attacked as a "white-eyed wolf and a fox who could no longer

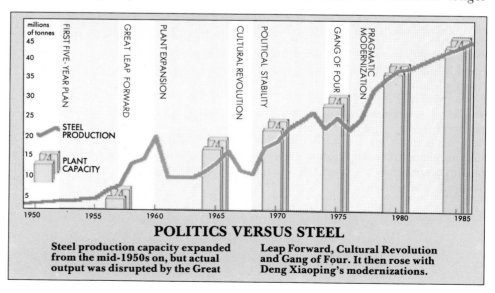

POLITICS VERSUS STEEL

Steel production capacity expanded from the mid-1950s on, but actual output was disrupted by the Great Leap Forward, Cultural Revolution and Gang of Four. It then rose with Deng Xiaoping's modernizations.

hide his tail''. A colleague, a young economics instructor, prudently did not speak out in public, but confided his doubts about the CCP's administrative skills to his girlfriend. Her careless gossip meant that he spent the next 15 years in labour camps.

After a brief but frightening period of repression, Mao loosed a second wave of socio-economic turbulence—the Great Leap Forward—which swept across China in 1958. Mao, a peasant's son, believed China could advance swiftly to economic power and into a purer form of egalitarian socialism by mobilizing the peasantry and applying this immense human resource (80 per cent of the population) to the nation's needs. In agriculture, this meant the organization of huge communes to replace traditional styles of living and working. In industry, it meant sudden decentralization and diversification. Both meant defeat for the go-slow rightists—the pragmatists, technocrats and experienced managers.

The Great Leap began in the winter of 1957-58, when 100 million peasants were put to work building dams and irrigation systems. By spring, communes had been organized and farmers were ploughing and planting to meet new production goals handed down by the party. People ate in mess halls, and the old folks tended communal nurseries, freeing the wives for farm work.

A central part of Mao's vision was the idea of self-sufficiency, which had preoccupied him since the 1930s. He maintained that each province—indeed, each village—should produce not only the food it needed, but also the other goods it would use. All sorts of small collective factories came to life, making pumps, tools, farm machinery. Farmers dug up their fields,

The disastrous Great Leap Forward (1958–60) was an attempt to boost production with cottage industry, including these backyard blast furnaces, which had antiquated mechanical blowers. The failure of the Leap almost ruined the economy.

5

seeking coal for the tiny backyard steel furnaces—little more than hot pyramids of brick—that became the Great Leap's most famous, if not most successful, feature.

Mao's obsession with self-sufficiency extended to the choice of crops. Announcing that "grain is the key link", he urged concentration on basic foodstuffs above all other products. Millions of farmers filled in fish ponds—a major source of essential protein—to plant rice, or abandoned soy beans and peanuts to plant wheat even where it would not grow.

The Great Leap Forward proved a catastrophe for China and its people. In the rush to speed production, the need for experience and skill and foresighted planning was ignored. When the hastily made farm machines broke down, there were no spare parts. Neither soy beans nor peanuts—resources of oils critical to the Chinese diet—were to be had. Dams built in haste, and without benefit of adequate hydrographic surveys, raised water tables, causing the surrounding land to become too alkaline or too salty to be of any use. Coal pits dug in fields left arable land an infertile ruin. Some of the backyard blast furnaces endured, although the pig iron they produced was of questionable value; others, made of soft adobe brick, crumbled in the rain.

Compounding this man-made havoc, the climate turned capricious, and 1959 and 1960 were marked by alternating periods of drought and flood made worse by insect infestation. Famine as of old descended upon the land, although it was not revealed until long afterwards that during the three years of the Great Leap there were an abnormal 16.5 million deaths,

mostly from starvation or diseases associated with malnutrition.

Appalled, Mao withdrew from active direction of affairs of state. He left the task of repairing the damage to his heir apparent, Vice Chairman Liu Shaoqi, assisted by Premier Chou En-lai and a rising younger official who was to become a principal actor in the dramas to follow, Deng Xiaoping.

Mao did not remain on the sidelines for long. He was galvanized into action when an old comrade in arms, Defence Minister Peng Dehuai, rashly dared to stand up and damn the master's policies. Never before had any leadership figure, obviously speaking with the support of a powerful faction, voiced criticism of Mao. Equally distressing to Mao were the pragmatic actions of Liu Shaoqi and Deng Xiaoping. To rebuild from the wreckage left by the Great Leap, they brought back merit rewards at work, downgraded the unwieldy communes and restored the powers of experienced managers. "It does not matter whether a cat is black or white," said Deng; "so long as it catches mice it is a good cat."

Mao began to criticize "those within the party who take the capitalist road". He turned against Liu Shaoqi and complained that Deng Xiaoping never consulted him. "I was being treated like a dead ancestor," he snapped.

Mao's domestic concerns were exacerbated by fears of yet another of the foreign incursions that have traumatized China over the millennia. Disputes with India, made worse by a revolt in Tibet, led to border clashes in 1959 and a short war, won by China in 1962. But the real threat appeared to come from the once-friendly Soviet Union. After several years of deteriorating relations—worsened by

Russian disapproval of the Great Leap Forward—Moscow in 1960 pulled out the teams of technicians that had been helping to modernize China, and cut off further economic and military aid.

Shocked by this rebuff from China's giant neighbour and fearing it might be followed by a Soviet invasion, Mao rallied the power of his political allies and sought to ensure the loyalty of the Army as well. Purging the doubting Peng Dehuai, Mao replaced him with Lin Biao, a marshal who in the civil war had commanded an army. Lin swiftly ordered a programme of political education designed to turn every soldier in China's huge military machine into a dedicated left-wing Communist.

The successful politicization of the People's Liberation Army (PLA) led Mao to seek the same goal throughout the rest of Chinese society. In the autumn of 1965 Mao, secure in his military support, decided to bring the capitalist roaders to heel once and for all. The Great Proletarian Cultural Revolution was to be a thoroughgoing purge of the elitists, inside and outside the CCP. Its aim was the ideal of state socialism—an absolutely egalitarian nation operated by the masses and rigidly controlled by the party.

For so shattering a convulsion, the Cultural Revolution appears to have been triggered by an event of small consequence: a play. A Peking playwright, Wu Han, wrote a drama called *Hai Jui Dismissed from Office*. Set in the 16th century, the play purported to tell of a palace functionary of the Ming Dynasty who was unjustly hounded from office by an autocratic Emperor. The leftists, with Mao's acquiescence, attacked it as a rightist allegory slandering the Chairman for getting rid of Defence Minister Peng.

Anti-Western propaganda climaxed during the Cultural Revolution with street drama, such as this parade, that ridiculed American stereotypes, including Uncle Sam *(centre)*. The placard denounces the Vietnam War.

The play was banned as subversive by Mao's wife Jiang Qing, an actress who had gained influence over the arts and who eventually became a dominant leftist figure in the Cultural Revolution, rising to the status of China's cultural dictator and exercising total rule over what might be written, painted, published or exhibited on stage or screen. At the peak of her power she had reduced the nation's allowable artistic expressions to six approved revolutionary ballets or operas.

The attack on playwright Wu Han was the initial gust of a tempest. Many schools and universities were closed, and political education sessions replaced other courses in those that stayed open. The educated—teachers, writers, artists, musicians, technicians, scientists—were stripped of their jobs and eventually dispersed to the fields of remote villages.

The youth were advised that it was "right to rebel", even against revisionists within the party, and were exhorted to "bombard the headquarters". Released from classes, they coalesced into vigilant bands of reformers. Before long, they had taken on a semblance of national organization, calling themselves the Red Guards.

Given free rides on the railways and supplied with food and lodging wherever they went, hordes of Red Guards charged from city to city—the first, and possibly the last, opportunity for ordinary Chinese to travel freely and see their great country. On August 18, 1966, close to a million of them converged on Peking's Tiananmen Square, where they were reviewed by Lin Biao and Mao himself, standing on top of the Gate of Heavenly Peace and wearing the red armband the Guards had adopted as their badge.

The officially approved targets of the Red Guards were "bourgeois elements", but as the young men and women with red armbands spread across the nation they were seized by mass hysteria. A campaign for reform became licence for destruction. A Red Guard leader in Peking proclaimed their new aim: "To create chaos and make a tremendous mess, the bigger

5

the better." With Mao's blessing and the approval of the Army—ordered by Lin Biao to "support the left"—they proceeded to make a mess. No issue was too slight; they even campaigned to have traffic light systems switched around so that red would mean "Go".

But most of their efforts were devoted to wholesale destruction of reputations and careers, a mass campaign of vengeance by the uprooted young against their established elders. One favourite weapon was the political poster. Peking's ancient city walls, and public buildings all over the country, were lurid with pictorial indictments. But in the end the denunciations came off the walls and became distinctly personal. To exercise their displeasure the Guards adopted a new definition of the word "struggle". "Struggle" no longer meant a contest between opposing forces, but a relentless inquisition that ended up destroying someone.

A professor being struggled by former students, for example, would be called into political sessions to explain and interpret the ideology of Chairman Mao. The teacher would be pressed to confess "crimes" against the revolution, and the individual who could not remember genuine misdeeds was well-advised to invent some. The miscreant might be forced to put on a dunce's cap or, if incautious enough to appear wearing a Western suit, the trousers would be scissored off at the knees to make Chinese-style shorts. Driven from the classroom, the accused teacher would be put to work cleaning toilets. One aged professor, with terminal cancer, was interrogated 22 separate times until he finally died. Another was beaten for inability to quote Mao precisely.

Professors were not the only ones to

suffer. A prominent engineer became a victim of the Red Guards after imprudently confiding to a chauffeur that Western can openers were more efficient than those made in China. One of China's foremost pianists, himself a Red Guard, had his hands broken when he got into a factional dispute with other Guards.

How all this tumult looked from the inside was recounted long afterwards by a young translator who worked in a government bureau in Peking, rendering English-language periodicals into Chinese and also translating Chinese press releases into English.

His fellow workers had enjoyed their jobs before the Cultural Revolution burst upon them. Most of the staff lived in dormitories in their office building. The pace was leisurely; the employees brewed tea at their desks and whiled away siesta hours playing chess or badminton on the roof. The translator had access to the outside world, reading such journals as *Time, Newsweek* and *The New York Times*.

The director, a man named Fu, was

an "old revolutionary", a high-ranking cadre with a chauffeur-driven car and a house furnished with such scarce luxuries as a private telephone and a refrigerator. Still, he seemed modest and hard-working, and the staff got along well with him.

One of the two assistant directors was another matter. "Fang was an arrogant son of a bitch," the translator recalled, "who took advantage of his rank to lord it over his subordinates. We used to call him Emperor Fang behind his back. He cultivated an ascetic image in public and deliberately rode his wife's bicycle to work each day to show that he was a modest man. It looked ridiculous, this tall, grey-haired, well-dressed cadre riding on this woman's small bicycle."

But Fang nevertheless had his bourgeois flaws. He wore a costly Swiss watch that he liked to flash in front of his underlings. His children, although only in their teens, already had their own bicycles, each then costing the equivalent of four months of an average labourer's pay.

Emperor Fang aside, the only distasteful part of the job was the four-times-a-week round of political indoctrination meetings. "We were bored at these meetings," the translator recalled, because he and his colleagues spent much of their time "reading and writing and translating these very same slogans." The ideology sessions were also dangerous. Even before the Cultural Revolution began, the staff tried to avoid being singled out for an opinion; those who were expressed only vague, safe views.

Caution remained the watchword for some time after the Cultural Revolution was announced. When it became clear, however, that Mao's—

Wearing face masks to protect them from the Gobi Desert dust that constantly swirls through Peking, school-age Red Guards read from Mao's "Little Red Book" *(opposite)* in a Cultural Revolution campaign denouncing "bourgeois elements".

MAO'S LITTLE RED BOOK

Clues to the origins of the Cultural Revolution can be found in modern China's most famous volume, the "Little Red Book" (9 by 14.5 cm) of quotations from Chairman Mao. Excerpts appear below.

● Dust will accumulate if a room is not cleaned regularly, our faces will get dirty if they are not washed regularly. Our comrades' minds and our Party's work may also collect dust, and also need sweeping and washing. The proverb "Running water is never stale and a door-hinge is never worm-eaten" means that constant motion prevents the inroads of germs and other organisms.

● A revolution is not a dinner party, or writing an essay, or painting a picture, or doing embroidery; it cannot be so refined, so leisurely and gentle, so temperate, kind, courteous, restrained and magnanimous. A revolution is an insurrection, an act of violence by which one class overthrows another.

● Not to have a correct political point of view is like having no soul.

● The outstanding thing about China's people is that they are "poor and blank". This may seem a bad thing, but in reality it is a good thing. Poverty gives rise to a desire for change, the desire for action and the desire for revolution.

● All reactionaries are paper tigers. In appearance, the reactionaries are terrifying, but in reality they are not so powerful.

and the Cultural Revolution's—primary target was Liu Shaoqi, his followers and other rightists, leftist activity in the bureau heated up. Soon the dining hall was so crowded with posters strung from wires that there was no room to eat. Some, such as those calling the benign Director Fu an "agent of Liu and a daring warrior of the black headquarters", struck the young translator as both cruel and illogical. But he enjoyed a measure of spiteful satisfaction when the posters attacked Fang and the other assistant director, a man named Ma. Both were repeatedly struggled, forced to confess to numerous anti-proletarian crimes and exiled to the countryside.

But then the bureau split into two warring factions, each claiming to be the true interpreter of Chairman Mao's thoughts. Slightly to the right were the more moderate staff members, who called themselves the Red Alliance. To the left were the extreme radicals, called the Red Flag. Spokesman for the moderates was Zhong, a party member and grade-17 cadre—the equivalent of a county magistrate. A thoughtful man in his forties, he was nicknamed the Theorist for his wide knowledge of Marxist theory. The Red Flag leader was another party member, Bao, a young ex-soldier who wore his uniform to work and was called the Imitation General.

The Imitation General quickly got the upper hand and began to detect enemies among his office mates. One he attacked for eating eggs—it was, he said, "a waste of state resources"—although Bao himself swiftly used his newly won power to improve his own standard of living, confiscating the flat of one of the deposed deputy directors, buying a bicycle and a wrist

watch, and spending money on women. He and others of the Red Flag singled out one Red Alliance member, an elderly man named Shao, for special denunciation and locked him in a third-floor room. Shao fell from the window and was killed. The Red Alliance believed Bao pushed him.

Bao turned on the translator as one of the "stinking bourgeois elements" to be attacked. "He personally supervised my own struggle and criticism at the hands of the Red Flag masses. I was accused of the basic crime of belonging to the Red Alliance," the translator recalled. "I was frog-marched into the dining hall one day and given a verbal and physical beating. The Imitation General was right in the middle, egging them on."

The leftist Red Flag faction won control of the bureau from the Red Alliance, and Zhong the Theorist was forced to concoct a confession and was struggled in a mass meeting. Banished to the country, he had a parting message for the translator. "They knocked me down," he said. "They called me a class enemy and trampled on my faith in Chairman Mao. But I will wait ten thousand years for my revenge."

He did not need to wait that long. After a few months the pendulum swung to the right and it was the Imitation General's turn to be struggled, bullied and disgraced.

Looking back, the English translator was moved to speak of the confusing terror of the Cultural Revolution in terms of an old Chinese proverb: kill the chickens to scare the monkeys. That is, do away with some less important people to cow the powerful ones. "They killed the chickens," the translator noted, "but did they really scare the monkeys? Well, that's hard to

5

answer and depends on who the monkeys really were. I had thought Bao and Zhong were the monkeys, but they turned out to be chickens like us."

Chicken and monkeys alike fell victim. One of the first and surely the most prominent was Mao's old companion Liu Shaoqi. Branded the chief revisionist by Mao himself, Liu was also attacked because his wife had received a Western-style education. Liu Shaoqi was dismissed from his posts, expelled from the CCP, banished to Kaifeng in Henan province and held under guard until he died of pneumonia in 1969. His wife was sent to Qincheng prison and forbidden by her jailers to speak to fellow inmates.

Other notables also suffered. Following Liu's downfall, Deng Xiaoping was turned out of his job and was reportedly sent off to learn humility as a mess-hall waiter. Even the respected, trusted Premier Chou En-lai was not immune. Despite his exalted status, he was unable to save his only child, Sun Weishi, a daughter adopted by Chou after her father had been killed in the 1930s. A theatrical director, she was arrested and sent to Qincheng prison in March 1968; seven months later she died there after being tortured.

Nobody kept count of the victims. Many, tortured or humiliated beyond bearing, killed themselves, one professor by plunging into a boiling hot spring in Fujian province. At the Qincheng prison, 500 party leaders were jailed; of these, 34 were tortured to death, 20 were permanently maimed and 60 were driven insane.

Such a wave of terror and purposeless destruction could not long continue. Before it ended, however, mob violence reached a crescendo. In Peking, Red Guards attacked and burnt the British Embassy. In early 1967, a mob stormed the Foreign Ministry, destroyed some archives, carried away others, and attempted but failed to kidnap the Foreign Minister. Near Chongqing, warring factions confronted each other in boats on the Jialing River; one force succeeded in ramming and sinking the other's vessel and then backed off while 200 people drowned. Rival gangs fought to the death with knives, clubs, battering rams and weapons taken from the Army—including, in one instance, an anti-aircraft gun.

A crucial confrontation in July of 1967 proved to be the turning point and took place in Wuhan, an industrial city and railway centre on the Yangtze. There the radicals—a mixture of younger industrial workers and student Red Guards calling themselves the Wuhan Workers' General Headquarters—were besieged within the city by the Million Heroes, a rightist guerrilla army, half a million strong, made up of skilled senior workers, civil service employees and militiamen.

The Million Heroes had the support of the Red Guards' natural enemies, the entrenched local officials. But in this instance they also had the backing of the regional Army commander, General Chen Zaidao. For a change, the Army—which had been the mainstay of radicalism—suddenly turned on the Red Guards it had consistently supported and protected. A battle broke out that threatened to escalate into civil war.

General Chen's stand in favour of the Heroes amounted to outright mutiny, for the Army was under orders from Peking to support the rebel left. Premier Chou En-lai, generally the peacemaker and mediator between left and right, dispatched orders to Chen to lift the siege. Chen ignored the orders. Chou dispatched two distinguished emissaries—one the Minister of Public Security—to deliver the directive in person. On July 19 the messengers instructed Chen and his officers to withdraw their backing of the Million Heroes. Instead, compounding the mutiny, Chen arrested the two envoys, one of whom was beaten up by soldiers at an Army headquarters. Desperate, Premier Chou flew to Wuhan to try to settle the matter in person. He failed; Chen had the airport ringed with tanks and troops and Chou's aircraft could not land.

For the first time in months, the demoralized and disorganized government in Peking acted decisively. Three infantry divisions, an airborne unit and a force of river gunboats moved in on the mutineers. General Chen and his rebellious officers were arrested and temporarily disgraced.

Chen appeared to have failed, but his aborted revolt changed the political climate. Once again Chairman Mao had seen all the destructive chaos he was willing to tolerate, at least for the moment. It was time to restore order and curb the rambunctious Red Guards. The Army was ordered to break up the bands and round up their members. Some 18 million Guards were sent off to the hinterland to be re-educated at hard labour.

The Red Guards' campaign of terror was virtually over, but Army Chief Lin Biao, vigorously supported by the radical coterie of Mao's wife, Jiang Qing, fought to pursue the egalitarian aims of the revolution of the masses. Mao, swinging from the far left back towards the centre, was apparently miffed by Lin's actions. He may have begun to doubt the loyalty of the PLA—he was heard to criticize the arrogance of the military. Then outside pressures deepened the rift between Lin and Mao. Alarmed by Russia's interference with its neighbours—skirmishes near the Ussuri River on the Sino-Soviet border and the Soviet invasion of Czechoslovakia—Mao looked westwards. He accepted a new policy of "peaceful coexistence and the establishment of friendly relations between states with different social systems"—that is, between China and the United States and Western Europe.

To Lin Biao this seemed a betrayal of the principles he had fought for. Banking on his stature as Mao's appointed heir, he made a fatal bid for power. He proposed to canonize Mao as a "genius" in a new constitution presented at the 1969-70 Party Congress.

Mao hastened to disavow this transparent attempt to shunt him aside, saying, "Genius does not depend on one person or a few people. It depends on a party." A year later, shortly after the announcement of an impending visit to China by U.S. President Nixon, Lin Biao disappeared. He was never again seen in public. The following year a government communiqué stated that the former Defence Minister, his family and certain political associates had died in a plane crash in Mongolia while attempting to escape, it was claimed, after the discovery of a coup that was to include the assassination of Mao Tse-tung.

Even before Lin Biao met his death, accidentally or otherwise, the rule of reason had begun to return to China. Schools and universities reopened. Thousands of exiled teachers, technocrats, managers and experts of all kinds, with skills vital to the nation's progress, were reinstated in their old jobs. Among those who returned were Director Fu, his deputies Fang and Ma, and the leaders of the warring factions of the Peking translation bureau; by 1973 Zhong the Theorist, who had vowed to wait ten thousand years for revenge, was working coldly but cooperatively alongside his former

enemy, the Imitation General. Eventually, according to official figures, 2.9 million people were rehabilitated.

Yet the curtain did not come down on the Cultural Revolution until Chairman Mao died, on September 9, 1976, aged 82. A brief, bitter struggle ensued at the top. This time the right won a clear victory. On October 6, China's new rulers opened a campaign to rid themselves of the left's most radical elements. The first to be struck down were the Gang of Four—Jiang Qing and her three closest associates. They were arrested, put on trial before TV cameras and sent to prison.

In the manoeuvring for power that followed, Deng Xiaoping emerged as China's paramount leader. Having

been ousted from power in 1969, rehabilitated by Chou En-lai in 1973 and then once more stripped of his posts by the Gang of Four, Deng had bitter personal experience of the Cultural Revolution. Once he had consolidated his position, he announced a startling shift away from class struggle; in his "Second Revolution", the emphasis would be on transforming China's economy by encouraging the "Four Modernizations"—of agriculture, industry, science and technology, and defence. Abandoning the Maoist ideal of a self-sufficient China, Deng initiated an "open door" policy, not only importing machinery but also encouraging Sino-foreign ventures and allowing thousands of students to go abroad

to study science, technology and even business management techniques.

Inevitably, these moves aroused public hopes of parallel political reforms, and provoked opposition from some of Deng's colleagues, who feared that the abandonment of long-held socialist tenets would undermine the power of the CCP. Deng, however, had no intention of yielding up the party's dominant position. "We cannot do without dictatorship," he declared.

In 1979 he ordered a crackdown on dissidents after posters appeared in Peking claiming that real economic prosperity could not be achieved unless the "Fifth Modernization"—democracy—was adopted. Dissent swelled again in 1986, when posters attacking China's leadership once more appeared on Peking's Democracy Wall, the main forum for China's pro-democracy movement. "I had no idea that in their eyes the people counted for nothing," one poster said. "They carry out their 'reforms'. But if you want to participate and if those reforms develop to the point where their interests are in danger, what do they give you?"

The democracy movement received its answer in June 1989.

In the intervening years, Deng's economic reforms had gone sour. Ordinary citizens were complaining openly about soaring inflation and widespread corruption. But the flashpoint of the crisis was the death, in April 1989, of Hu Yaobang, a former Party General-Secretary sacked for allegedly supporting the students in the protests of 1986.

On April 22, the day of Hu's funeral, 100,000 demonstrators occupied Tiananmen square, calling for the dismissal of Deng and other veteran leaders.

The security forces did not intervene. Within the Party hierarchy there were factions who supported some of the protestors' demands, and even hardliners were reluctant to order a display of force only a few weeks before a Sino-Soviet summit intended to mark the formal reconciliation of the world's leading communist powers.

In fact, the visit of Soviet president Mikhail Gorbachev was severely disrupted by the demonstrators, who by now were staging a hunger strike in the square. Party General-Secretary Zhao Ziyang went in person to plead with them to leave, and openly admitted that the students had a right to criticize the leadership. But Deng, supported by hardline premier Li Peng and other conservative colleagues, had already decided on a military solution. Once Gorbachev had departed, the government lost no time in imposing martial law and calling in the PLA to clear the square.

Incredibly, the army's advance was blocked in the suburbs by citizens who flooded on to the streets and hectored the bemused soldiers. For two weeks, the army remained stalled on Peking's outskirts, while in Tiananmen Square the students erected a 10-metre-high statue provocatively called the "Goddess of Democracy".

By June Zhao Ziyang and his faction within the leadership had lost the power struggle to the hardliners. Another assault on the square, on June 2, again failed dismally—possibly a deliberate manoeuvre to justify the full-blooded attack mounted on the following night.

As darkness fell on June 3, soldiers broke through road blocks and converged on Tiananmen, shooting at random. After reaching the square, they held their fire while the demonstrators made a negotiated withdrawal, but once the sacred site was cleared, the soldiers turned withering fire on anyone who appeared in their sights. All that night and the next day the shooting continued.

Several hundred people were killed in Peking alone, and thousands of "counter-revolutionaries" were arrested in the months that followed. In order to root out "deviant" individuals, political re-education was introduced once more into the workplace. The near-dormant network of informers was revived, together with the practice of placing little information boxes in the entrance to every workplace, where anonymous accusations against colleagues could be posted. Students were confined to campus and many were extensively interrogated; six months after the euphemistically termed "June Event", Chinese newspapers briefly reported a number of suicides among those who had participated in the protests.

The bloody suppression was intended as a clear signal that the regime would not tolerate political reform or any challenge to its authority. The communist old guard had no intention of opening a dialogue with young students whom they considered ungrateful for the sacrifices made by the revolutionary veterans. The issue of loyalty crucial to Chinese politics was again defined as unquestioning obedience to the CCP. And yet the events leading up to the massacre indicated that the fundamental disagreements which had plagued the Party under Mao were still there, still tugging left and right, creating perilous cracks within the seeming monolith.

At the height of anti-government demonstrations in 1989, one of the young protestors occupying Peking's Tiananmen Square raises his arms in a gesture of triumph. A week later, hope gave way to tragedy as the Army stormed the square, then opened fire on demonstrators and bystanders alike.

On a railway journey, officers of the People's Liberation Army ride first-class, one of many privileges they enjoy. The Army holds the balance of political power within China.

THE SYSTEM: RULES MADE TO BE BENT

Soon after the introduction of Deng Xiaoping's economic reforms in the late 1970s, a Texan businessman trading in oil equipment arrived in Peking to arrange the sale of drilling parts to a Chinese government corporation. The negotiations were almost complete when he was told: "There is just one more thing we need. The deal will cost you 2 per cent of the value of the sale." The money, added the official, was to be deposited in a numbered bank account in Switzerland. The American was astounded. It appeared to be a demand for a bribe—the kind of corruption that might be expected in some of the more free-wheeling countries of Asia, but certainly not in puritanical, socialist China.

The demand was technically illegal, but in this case the Chinese official did not want the money for himself. It was part of a scheme that enabled the corporation to function more efficiently. Obtaining equipment through government channels was a maddeningly slow process, encumbered by red tape. And sometimes parts were simply unavailable in China. The secret account existed to finance purchase of equipment overseas, sidestepping scarcities and governmental delays at home.

The Texan's experience illustrates an unexpected truth about China today. The people of one of the most tightly regimented systems on earth—one which attempts to dictate virtually every aspect of daily life—show a sur-

prisingly materialistic independence and initiative. They know they must go along with the system, but they—and their leaders—recognize that the rules can be bent. "Our minds are on the left," goes a Chinese saying, "but our pockets are on the right."

The centrepiece of that system, the Chinese Communist Party, dominates life from the top down. It is theoretically separate from the government, but its key officials are also key government officials, and it sets the policies that the government carries out. At the top is the General Secretary, who heads the major decision-making body of the party. The CCP's members occupy leadership positions in all the important government institutions, even on a local level. The party also holds ultimate authority over the People's Liberation Army. This huge force has 1.5 million combat troops and about the same number of support troops. It runs its own scientific and technical institutes, farms and factories, plus more than 100 military academies and hospitals.

The CCP nominates the country's premier, who is then approved by the rubber-stamp National People's Congress. The premier in turn presides over the State Council, which is made up of the three dozen or so ministries that conduct the country's economic activities, foreign-policy negotiations, overseas trade, internal security and even cultural affairs. Party members at

6

every echelon of government make sure all agencies follow the party line. Even in remote farm villages, party members take charge of the people's social and economic lives.

Two elites have arisen in this otherwise egalitarian society. Few members of either live in luxury, but they do enjoy some perquisites unavailable to the average farmer or factory worker. These elites are the PLA and the party.

About 45 million people—only 4 per cent of China's population—belong to the party. Getting in is difficult. A candidate must have a "good class background": no child or even grandchild of a one-time rich landlord need apply. Would-be party members must also demonstrate ideological zeal and endure a year-long probationary period that may include writing down virtually everything they do or think. One woman whose husband managed to win party membership said that he "had to put on a big show of being hard-working and making sacrifices". In addition, he had to *pai ma pi*—"pat the horse's rump", that is, curry favour with his local party secretary.

Joining the party also entails real risks—of espousing the party's official line today only to find tomorrow that the line has changed. The result of being politically out of step in the past has included long terms in labour camps for "political re-education". Yet, the rewards for party membership are considerable: better jobs, faster promotions and access to special shops, resorts and medical care. Many young Chinese are willing to run the risks for the chance of a better life.

Second only to the party, the PLA conveys special power and prestige to its members. Technically, all Chinese males are subject to conscription at the age of 18, but most ranks are filled by volunteers. A handful of young female volunteers also are enlisted.

Those accepted into the PLA were once considered fortunate indeed. Rations were better than a peasant's average fare. Uniforms were at least warm, if hardly prepossessing—and of the same style, without insignia of rank, for generals and privates. In recent years these advantages have held less attraction as food and other comforts have become more plentiful. However, a young soldier acquires status and opportunities not available to everyone. For one thing, the PLA is a significant force in the country's economic life, cultivating its own farms and producing its own consumer goods. Many conscripts therefore receive on-the-job training in agricultural techniques and industrial skills.

But perhaps the greatest advantage of military service is the opportunity offered to gain party membership. Although universities, offices and factories have quotas for party membership, the military has proportionately the largest quota. If a soldier fails to win acceptance by the party during his tour of duty, he probably never will.

One young soldier was so upset by party rejection that he attended his unit's passing-out banquet with a hand

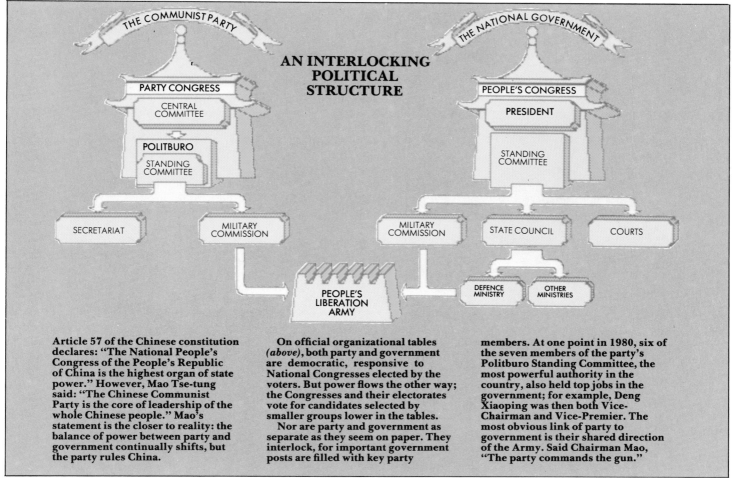

AN INTERLOCKING POLITICAL STRUCTURE

THE COMMUNIST PARTY

PARTY CONGRESS

CENTRAL COMMITTEE

POLITBURO

STANDING COMMITTEE

SECRETARIAT

MILITARY COMMISSION

THE NATIONAL GOVERNMENT

PEOPLE'S CONGRESS

PRESIDENT

STANDING COMMITTEE

MILITARY COMMISSION

STATE COUNCIL

COURTS

DEFENCE MINISTRY

OTHER MINISTRIES

PEOPLE'S LIBERATION ARMY

Article 57 of the Chinese constitution declares: "The National People's Congress of the People's Republic of China is the highest organ of state power." However, Mao Tse-tung said: "The Chinese Communist Party is the core of leadership of the whole Chinese people." Mao's statement is the closer to reality: the balance of power between party and government continually shifts, but the party rules China.

On official organizational tables (*above*), both party and government are democratic, responsive to National Congresses elected by the voters. But power flows the other way; the Congresses and their electorates vote for candidates selected by smaller groups lower in the tables.

Nor are party and government as separate as they seem on paper. They interlock, for important government posts are filled with key party members. At one point in 1980, six of the seven members of the party's Politburo Standing Committee, the most powerful authority in the country, also held top jobs in the government; for example, Deng Xiaoping was then both Vice-Chairman and Vice-Premier. The most obvious link of party to government is their shared direction of the Army. Said Chairman Mao, "The party commands the gun."

grenade under his jacket. When his regimental commander proposed a farewell toast, he pulled the pin, killing himself and a dozen others.

The soldier's despair at the prospect of returning to the peasantry was understandable at the time. Since then, many things have changed for the better, yet farmers still must put in day after day of strenuous physical labour, little lightened by modern machinery. Before the 1949 Liberation, small plots were worked by tenant farmers who turned over much of their crops to landowners and officials. Some landowners were simply well-off peasants who had acquired fields in addition to those they tilled themselves, but many of the large tracts were

owned by absentee landlords. The great majority of tenant farmers gave up so much of their crops in rents and taxes that they barely subsisted in good times and starved in bad times.

After the Communist victory, the land was redistributed, but this has not led to government operation of farming in the Soviet pattern: only about 3 per cent of the arable area is tilled by salaried workers on state-owned farms. Chinese agriculture has become a complex mixture of official regulation and individual enterprise. Moreover, the balance between official direction through the party hierarchy and independent control by local farmers and managers has shifted dramatically with changes of political ideology.

In 1958, as the first step in China's Great Leap Forward, virtually all of China's farmers were organized into some 23,500 communes, averaging 5,000 households each. At first the communes were intended to be true collectives—homogeneous social units whose members shared all work and rewards equally. Private plots, where farmers might grow food to eat or sell, were condemned by Mao Tse-tung as "the tails of capitalism". He urged commune leaders to chop down the farmers' own fruit trees and rip out melon-patches. But the peasants did not take to such regimentation. Malingering became chronic and farm production sank alarmingly.

Since those early days, the system

Exuding confident authority, an Army officer is driven through a city street. He wears no insignia of rank, but his power is signalled by his bearing, by the tailoring of his uniform and by the gleaming vehicle.

123

6

has been liberalized, despite occasional swings the other way. By 1962, the original 23,500 communes had been split into 75,000, each subdivided into a dozen or so production brigades that, in turn, included a dozen or more production teams. Each team worked about 20 hectares with tools and seeds supplied by the commune. Under a leader (usually a party member) it determined—in consultation with the production brigade or commune—what was to be planted. Then it assigned to everyone a particular job, scheduled the work, produced the crop and, most important to members, decided how to split the profits.

How much a member earned was set by a fascinating system of accounting called *gong-fen*, or "work points"—credits exchangeable for food or cash. The number of work points received depended on the work done. A strong man received as many as 12 points for a day's work, while a woman of the same age might have been awarded only eight, and a child only half that.

The team's work-point recorder listed these credits and at the end of the year the team settled up. The plus side of the ledger included payments by the state at a fixed price for production of a state-set quota of food. The minus side included costs of production and payments to the commune or brigade for services such as education and medical care. The remainder was divided among members on the basis of accumulated points. Also, peasants were allowed to keep produce from private garden plots, restored as an incentive in the early 1960s.

In theory the commune system was egalitarian, but in practice the realistic assessment of work points caused too much strife, so the team leaders were tempted to narrow the differentials. Favouritism was also shown towards relatives and friends, and peasants resented the high number of bonus work-points allocated to party cadres who did no productive work. In Tibet, where the commune system was fully implemented by 1970, peasants were reduced to a starvation diet. "Liberation is like having a wet leather cap put on one's head," they said. "The quicker it dries, the tighter it gets, until it kills you."

With minor variations, the commune system survived until the end of the 1970s when, in the first wave of Deng Xiaoping's economic reforms, it was gradually replaced by the so-called responsibility system. Under the new rules, first production teams consisting of three to five families, then individual households, were made the unit of production. Each work unit still had to meet a fixed production quota but was allowed to keep anything produced over and above the quota to use as its own or to sell at the roadside or in the burgeoning free markets.

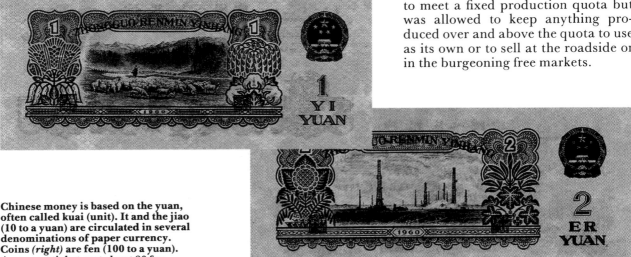

Chinese money is based on the yuan, often called kuai (unit). It and the jiao (10 to a yuan) are circulated in several denominations of paper currency. Coins *(right)* are fen (100 to a yuan). A concert ticket cost about 80 fen, a restaurant meal two yuan.

To encourage greater investment, the government allotted land to the peasants on a rental basis, and even allowed them to hire labour. At first the peasants were supposed to rotate the land every few years, but in 1984—when the system had been applied to more than 90 per cent of rural areas—the length of tenure was fixed at 15 years. In 1987, peasants were given a guarantee that the rental contract would be increased to 50 years, and that children could inherit their rights. Only by allowing land to pass from generation to generation, it was argued, could peasants be persuaded to make long-term investments.

The new system produced startling results almost at once; the 1984 grain crop was a record, 25 per cent up on 1978. As grain production soared, the government replaced the compulsory quota system with a more flexible procurement system. They also introduced incentives to diversify into cash crops and other sideline products.

The transformation of rural China has not been achieved without costs, however. The small scale of the new family enterprises has meant that there are not enough agricultural technicians to go round. With the virtual abolition of the commune, vital irrigation and drainage schemes previously maintained collectively have been allowed to fall into disrepair. Because the rural economy is largely in private hands, the government is faced with the problem of implementing a coherent investment strategy for agriculture. After the record grain crop of 1984, so many peasants abandoned their traditional crops for more lucrative ventures, such as fish farming and flower production, that grain production for 1985 was down by 7 per cent. Controls on grain production were reimposed, but although output has picked up, the early promise of huge increases has not been fulfilled.

The Chinese media devoted exaggerated attention to the agricultural boom, arousing the envy of townspeople with stories about the rural ''ten-thousanders''—families with an annual income of 10,000 yuan, about £3,800. But once the agricultural reforms were under way, it was the turn of the industrial sector. In the cities, where most of Chinese industry is located, the work is easier than on the farms and wages are generally better, but the web of government economic control has been much tighter. In the 1950s, small businesses were organized into collectives supervised by the state, while larger factories and all major industries were placed firmly under government control. Until the 1980s, the state not only established production quotas, as it did in agriculture, but also set basic wages and regulated marketing. The Chinese themselves used to complain loudly and often about inefficient use of industrial equipment, duplication of effort and needless loss of production. A glaring example is the Chinese motor-vehicle industry.

In 1980 a visiting team from the American Motors Corporation was surprised to find that China had no fewer than 130 car and truck

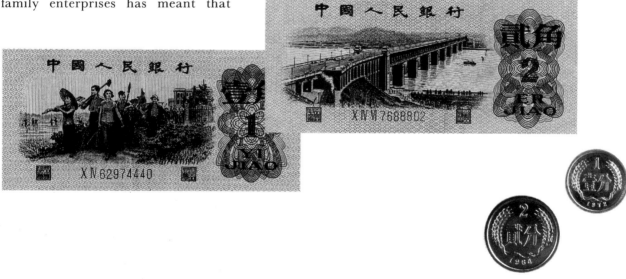

6

factories—the largest number in the world—but that they turned out only some 220,000 vehicles a year, about the number produced by AMC's two U.S. plants. The large number of plants can be traced in part to recent Chinese history. Mao believed in self-sufficiency. In the days of guerrilla warfare, every Red Army unit had to be self-contained, so every region manufactured its own cars and trucks.

When the Americans visited the factory of the largest car manufacturer in Peking, which made a small vehicle resembling AMC's own Jeep, they were again surprised to discover that, although capable of turning out 45,000 vehicles a year, it was producing only a third that number. The plant usually fulfilled its annual quota of 15,000 cars by September, then shut down for the rest of the year. The huge labour force of 9,700 workers stayed on—at full pay—maintaining the machinery. Even so, price rigging ensured a tidy profit. Each vehicle was sold for nearly 45 per cent more than the manufacturing cost; selling price and profit were 20 per cent higher than for a similar car in the West.

But the profit meant little to the factory. All but 5 per cent of it had to be handed over to central government. With the 5 per cent, the factory manager could award small bonuses to his workers, but could not raise their basic wages. Nor could he expand the plant and increase production without obtaining permission. According to the Chinese newspaper, *People's Daily*, when the head of a heavy-machinery plant in Shenyang wanted to build a dormitory to house workers he had to win permission from 11 separate government agencies and get 24 official chops, or seals, on the documents.

Using a metaphor derived from the fact that Chinese families are matriarchies, ruled by elderly women, the manager said his problem came from having too many "grandmothers".

Cutting back would have been as forbidding a task for the car plant manager as expanding. If he had wished to reduce costs, for example, he would have found it difficult to fire a significant number of workers. For years the People's Republic followed a system of employment security known as *tie fan wan*—"the iron rice bowl"—meaning a job for life, frequently handed on from parent to child. Since no one could be sacked, few employees worked hard; no matter how idle a factory might be, it was never closed.

Such complacency, together with excessive bureaucracy and state interference, was among the targets of Deng Xiaoping's economic reforms, promulgated in 1984 and designed to "bring about an all-round upsurge" of the economy. The essence of industrial reforms was a reduction of party involvement in the day-to-day running of state-owned enterprises. They would not be privatized, but as Premier Zhao Ziyang explained, their managers would be "truly independent, self-managing and solely responsible for their own profits". Managers could keep a much greater share of their factory's profit after paying a specified amount of tax to the state, and with this money they were able to award bonuses and, if they preferred, to pay piece-work rates rather than fixed day rates. They were also given limited powers to hire and fire and, in 1985, a contract system was introduced for new staff, ending—in theory at least—the job-for-life system.

Businesses such as restaurants, cob-blers and bicycle repair shops could now be leased outright by their managers. The result was an upsurge in the retail and service trade, the number of private owners and employees in this sector rising from 4 per cent in 1978 to nearly 50 per cent in 1986. For the first time in years, people could eat in a cheap restaurant without queuing.

Responding to the new entrepreneurial spirit, an aircraft factory in Xian opened a booming marriage introduction centre. A Guangdong university invested in a Shanghai bar, where one floor, called Lovers' World, was furnished with 15 banquettes for courting couples. One of Peking's luxury tourist hotels, the Palace, which has two gold-coloured Rolls-Royce Corniches available for special guests, is owned by the PLA.

In foreign trade, too, great advances were made. By 1989, the Chinese had licensed 10,000 joint-ventures with overseas companies—mainly in the four Special Economic Zones, which, according to a Chinese economist, would "act as filters between China's socialist system and the capitalist world." By the same year China had made use of more than U.S. $20 billion in foreign credits to import technology. In Peking, the Chairman of the New York Stock Exchange was given a warm reception, and foreign commentators proclaimed that China was becoming capitalist. This is not the case, however. By the late 1980s, the state sector still accounted for 95 per cent of the economy, which continued to operate according to a government-approved Five-Year Plan. Nor has the new emphasis on enterprise management been an unqualified success.

One of the main problems was wages. By Western standards, Chinese

workers' pay is low; in the mid-1980s, a factory manager or a professor earned about 100 yuan (£38) a month, a blue-collar worker about half that. But until the economic reforms took effect, cost of necessities was also low, because essential goods and services were heavily subsidized by the state. The average rent for a flat at the beginning of the 1980s amounted to little more than 1 per cent of family income, and staple foods were comparatively cheap. The cost of rice to urban consumers had remained unchanged since the founding of the People's Republic.

With the introduction of the bonus incentive scheme, urban workers' wages shot up, rising 68 per cent between 1981 and 1985. The government had intended that bonus payments be limited to some 10 per cent of basic wages, but this was soon breached, with many companies awarding across-the-board bonuses of up to one third of annual wages. This led to an inflationary consumption boom, heavily increasing the state's financial burden.

The obvious solution was to pass on the increased costs to the consumers, but the urban Chinese, long conditioned to stable, unchanging prices, regarded this as an unsocialist attack on their living standards. In 1988, with inflation running at more than 20 per cent—the highest since the overthrow of the Nationalist regime—the public reacted to price rises by embarking on a panic-buying spree, adding to the inflationary pressures which contributed to the political crisis of 1989.

Scarcity of goods, rather than of money, continues to plague the urban Chinese, for though industrial production has soared, distribution is uneven. Problems with quality also arises because most jobs are still assigned by the government, often with little regard for a person's qualifications or preferences. A quality-control officer at a Guangdong electronics factory admitted his own ineptitude. "I graduated in English," he said. "I don't know anything about the work here, so I can't judge product quality very well. I wish I could go somewhere else, but I may be stuck here for the rest of my life." One of the causes of the student

6

resentment that led to the Tiananmen demonstrations of 1989 was the government's reversal of a decision to scrap the job-allocation system.

Another source of popular resentment is the critical deficiency of living space: the average allotment of housing in Shanghai, for example, is some four square metres per person, about the equivalent of a king-sized bed. This space is usually in the form of a tiny one-room flat with no bathroom or kitchen. Those facilities are down the hall and are shared by neighbours.

Such cramped quarters lead to social difficulties. A recently married couple were asked how they managed their love life when, unable to acquire a flat of their own, they had moved into a one-room flat with the husband's mother and brother: they said the brother had obligingly taken up residence in the factory's dormitory for bachelors, and the mother had temporarily gone to stay with relatives.

Like shelter, the other basic necessity, food, is spartan. The average Chinese gets a reasonably balanced diet that gives adults about 2,000 calories per day. Many nutritionists consider this sufficient, though it is about two thirds the calorie intake of people in more affluent societies.

For most urban Chinese, simply acquiring supplies for this frugal fare is a formidable task. The shopper must pay in cash and carry half a dozen types of ration coupons for purchases ranging from rice to cooking oil to the soap for washing up. Most of all, shopping takes time. City dwellers may spend several hours every day just laying in necessities. Time-consuming delays are caused by the need to queue at several stores to assemble the ingredients for a single meal.

Since most meals include rice or a wheat product such as noodles, shopping trips regularly include a visit to a government-owned grain store. The size of the monthly allotment varies with age and occupation. A steelworker who performs heavy manual labour gets nearly twice as much as a female factory worker, and 10 times more than an infant. After the grain store comes the grocery shop, which sells other rationed staples such as eggs and sugar. No coupons are needed for fruit and vegetables at yet another shop, but the shopper must be prepared to choose from limited selections and to queue for each item.

Attractive alternatives to the state-owned shops are the free markets, where prices are higher but the range of goods is wider. In the countryside, these are usually held on regular dates based on the old rural 10-day week, and on market days the roads leading to the small towns are jammed with peasants carrying poultry, eggs, vegetables and fish wrapped in wet leaves to keep them alive. Urban markets are sufficiently profitable for peasants to travel up to 80 kilometres to them, sleeping overnight on their carts before the market opens in the morning.

Free markets, privately owned shops and urban collectives have also increased the availability of household items such as soap, cooking utensils, crockery and furniture. Near Canton, capital of Guangdong province, a stretch of road is lined with shops full of sofas, chairs and beds. "Furniture row" is not the brainchild of urban entrepreneurs, but was created by local farmers who decided to augment their income by making household goods. The market attracts custom from all over the province—wholesale buyers who resell the goods at a handsome profit, as well as householders wishing to furnish their own homes.

Of course, many Chinese cannot afford free market prices, and must still rely on the state rationing system and government subsidies. Only newlyweds are entitled to the three basic pieces of furniture—double bed, folding dining table and dresser-cabinet—and they may have to wait six months to receive them. While many Chinese homes now have fridges and colour televisions, the average household is fortunate if it possesses the "three rounds and a sound"—bicycle, sewing machine, watch and transistor radio. A bicycle is still a highly prized possession, indispensable for transport in a country where most cars are official vehicles. One of the most incongruous sights of modern Peking is the suited businessmen using cellular phones as they pedal to or from work.

CHINESE MEASURES

China uses the metric system in most of its international trade. For domestic transactions, however, the traditional Chinese units, listed below with the metric equivalent, are preferred.

Chinese Unit		Approximate Metric Equivalent
两	liang	50 grams
斤	jin	.5 kilogram
担	dan	60 kilograms
升	sheng	.5 litre
斗	dou	4.4 litres
斛	hu	53 litres
寸	cun	3 cm
尺	chi	.3 meter
里	li	.5 km
亩	mu	.06 hectare

Buying a bike is not easy, although China is the world's leading manufacturer (some 35 million a year). The price is high—about three months' wages for the average industrial worker—and collecting the necessary coupons takes years. Some shoddy models, however, can be purchased without coupons. "The shops are full of them," one of Peking's 3.6 million cyclists said. "But no one wants to buy rubbish like that. They fall apart in a couple of months."

There is one group—China's growing number of itinerants and migrant workers—who, for good or ill, live outside the rationing system, beyond official control. As the economic reforms gathered pace, large cities attracted floating populations of migrants from poorer areas; in some cities, these people make up 10 per cent of the population. They possess no residence permits, so are not entitled to ration cards or state benefits and must live by their wits, working on construction sites, helping out in the markets, in some cases resorting to begging. Some booming provinces, such as Guangdong, have turned a blind eye to the inflow of cheap labour—much to the aggravation of poorer neighbouring provinces, such as Hunan, which tried to stem the flow of its people by setting up roadblocks. In 1989, tens of thousands of itinerant labourers were forced to return to their home towns when the government cancelled hundreds of state construction projects in an attempt to curb excessive capital investment.

After June 1989, in fact, the cities lost some of their allure for rural workers seeking well-paid jobs. As part of a package of anti-inflation measures, it became compulsory for both factory and white-collar workers to purchase government bonds—just one example of the all-pervasive control exercised by the party.

Only a relatively small number of Chinese escape the day-by-day scrutiny of the state. The control mechanisms are not always evident to visitors, who often comment upon the casual contempt the Chinese show for their uniformed policemen. But uniformed police, and their plainclothes counterparts in the Public Security Bureau, are only the surface of an extremely complex security apparatus that monitors virtually every aspect of life. This apparatus, most powerful in the cities, has been described by a long-term resident of Peking as being "like radar; it picks you up wherever you go".

At the everyday level, control is maintained by three overlapping types of organization, none of them formally a part of the government structure. The most ubiquitous is the *danwei*, or work-place unit. Virtually every Chinese belongs to a *danwei* at a factory, office or school, and the *danwei* maintains a grip on many aspects of everyone's public and personal life. Changing jobs, getting a better flat, travelling overnight to another city, all require permission from the *danwei*. Slips of the tongue or untoward behaviour are certain to be noted in the confidential dossier kept on each individual. It contains everything the party needs to know, including an up-to-date evaluation of political soundness and detailing three generations of ancestors to establish class background. The *danwei* even regulates marriage and divorce. A couple wanting to marry must first meet state-ordained age requirements: the man must be at least 22 and the woman 20. (In the overcrowded cities, residents are urged to delay longer—men until 27, women until 25.) Then the couple must seek approval from the *danwei*. Often the man and woman belong to different work units in different parts of the country, and *danwei*-to-*danwei* negotiations have to be set in motion.

Marriage does not always end such separations. According to one estimate, job assignments force some four million couples to live apart. Lonely husbands and wives usually see each other—with *danwei* permission—only during the six national work holidays or during special 12-day leaves sometimes granted to those forced to live apart. Small handwritten notices offering exchange of jobs and housing aimed at reuniting couples can be seen on walls in every Chinese city. The stress of separation often leads to permanent estrangement. But divorce is surprisingly difficult to arrange. The state frowns upon it, and the work units try to reconcile differences.

While the *danwei* provides the primary mechanism of social and political control, a second group, the street committee, watches the daily lives of city dwellers even more closely. Every urban neighbourhood has its own committee, which provides residents with services such as day-care centres. In return, the committee subjects the personal lives of its parishioners to unremitting surveillance.

In each block of flats, the residents elect a representative to the street committee; usually they choose a woman. One such representative—ironically her name is Ma—has been vividly described by a Western correspondent. Ma was a rotund woman in her fifties who, in action, resembled a cross between a caretaker, police informant, social worker and "union-hall hiring boss". She kept a watchful eye on the housekeeping habits of all residents in her district and reprimanded laggards for not sweeping floors or unwashed dishes. She and members of the street committee developed the disconcerting habit of entering flats after midnight without knocking. Ostensibly there to check on the residents' *hukou*—the required household registration certificate—they were actually looking for strangers living in the flat illegally. "There is no way to be alone," one of her charges complained. "She even watches what time we go to bed. We are like caged animals."

It was, in fact, part of Ma's function to monitor bedroom behaviour. Since 1981, the Chinese government has followed a stringent birth-control policy, inspired by fear that the nation's people could outstrip the food supply and bring back the catastrophic famines of old. The policy aimed at reducing population growth to zero by the year 2000. Quotas for births are set by the government and enforced with incentives and penalties. One child is considered the maximum acceptable except in special cases. A couple with only one child may be rewarded with wage increases and preferences in admission to a school or hospital. Having two or more children may bring penalties, including fines and reduced food rations for the second child.

The government-set birth quotas are parcelled out at the local level by street committees such as Ma's. Childless couples usually get first priority. All others are monitored to see that they do not violate the priority system and contribute to a quota-breaking baby boom. The committees assign some

one to keep track of each woman's menstrual cycle. Said one committee member: "If someone misses her period and isn't scheduled to have a baby, we tell her to have an abortion. There isn't any room for liberalism on such an issue."

But love and sex occasionally triumph over the best efforts of the street committee or *danwei*. People do bear more children than they are supposed to, especially in the country, where family labour is a vital resource. One Sichuan woman was fined 1,300 yuan for having seven children. The first six were girls, but as she explained: "Girls are no use. They can't inherit your house or your property. Your daughters all marry out and belong to someone else." In some cases, parents desperate for a boy have killed their first child when it proved to be a girl.

If the laws are flouted, a citizen is at the mercy of a legal system in which the arbitrary dictates of individuals rather than rule of law prevail. China's Communist rulers have an ideological view of crime. They regard the offender as an errant child who needs re-educating back to responsible citizenship. Such paternalism is not new; in

imperial China a county magistrate was known as the *fu mu guan*—"the father and mother official".

In modern-day China, the perpetrator of a minor crime may never see a magistrate of any kind. Consider the case of a young person who offends a street committee by engaging in pre-marital sex. A group of local officials convenes—police, governmental authorities, perhaps someone from the street committee—and decides what to do with the offender. Without a trial or a chance to speak up in defence, the accused can be sentenced to up to three years of *laojiao*—re-education through labour.

This re-education takes place in special labour camps. In 1982, Western journalists were permitted to visit the Tuanhe Farm, a labour camp south of Peking with more than 2,000 inmates, all male. Although inmates ranged in age from 17 to 60, 87 per cent were under 25. More than half were guilty of petty thievery. Of the rest, a majority had been accused of "hooliganism"—a catch-all offence defined by the deputy director as "fighting that disturbs the peace, or taking liberties with women". But some prisoners

In a factory shop, a welder applies her torch as she works at a task often assigned to women because it does not require male strength. Though women make up nearly half the industrial labour force of China, they earn much less than men on average.

were guilty only of minor affronts to official morality; one was confined for playing cards for money, a traditional pastime forbidden in modern China.

In the 1980s, the field of minor offences was enlarged to take account of what Deng Xiaoping called "harmful elements of bourgeois culture imported from the West". In campaigns against so-called "spiritual pollution", women were ordered to have their hair cut short, soldiers were ordered to hand over photographs of their girlfriends, and young men were summarily dispossessed of their fashionable dark glasses.

Any citizen accused of a serious crime such as rape, murder or political deviance is caught up in what one Western scholar has characterized as "the nearest thing to the Inquisition in the contemporary world". The suspect is jailed with no provision for bail. Guilty by presumption, he or she is expected to express contrition through confession; to this end, jailers conduct interminable interrogations, using psychological intimidation, though rarely outright physical torture.

When the case comes to trial, the accused faces an official judge and two lay "assessors", who have perhaps a smattering of legal training, but no jury. Under a legal code approved in 1979—after three decades without one—the defendant now possesses certain rights not hitherto available: to have a lawyer (by the end of the 1980s, there were only 33,000 in all of China); to call witnesses and to cross-examine those of the prosecution; and to have a trial open to some of the public.

In practice, the verdict is almost always guilty, for a case is rarely brought to trial unless guilt has been established to the satisfaction of both the prosecution and the court. After the trial, the defendant may appeal the verdict to the next highest court in China's four-tier judicial structure. But defendants seldom exercise this right. An appeal indicates lack of contrition and often results in a stiffer sentence.

Most of those convicted of serious crimes are sent to labour camps usually much harsher than the re-education farms for minor offenders; some are in remote frontier regions such as the bitterly cold and barren Qinghai province. Few outsiders have seen these camps. The government refuses to discuss how many prisoners inhabit them. Estimates range from several hundred thousand to several million. Former inmates tell of starvation diets; gruelling work in mines, quarries and forests; and endless sessions devoted to ideological reform.

Most inmates never return home after completing their sentences. "It would always be on your dossier," said one. "You couldn't get a decent job, and you'd have trouble finding a wife." After their release, most remain on the fringes of the camps, receiving regular wages for their labour, marrying and raising families.

For years, the Chinese Communists claimed they had virtually eliminated serious crime, but while there may once have been some truth in this, it no longer has credibility in modern-day China. And prostitution, virtually eradicated during the early Maoist era, has returned, bringing a sharp increase in venereal diseases.

Robberies, rape and murder have become everyday occurrences. In 1988, the overall crime rate was up by 45 per cent on 1987, which had seen a 25 per cent increase over the previous year. Serious crimes rose by 65 per cent—to 120,000—in 1987. Clearly the government decided to set a harsh example, for in 1988 an estimated 10,000 criminals were summarily executed by means of a bullet in the back of the head, the usual Chinese way of carrying out the death penalty.

The majority of serious offences against the state during this period were "economic" crimes, committed by individuals who had followed the government's "get rich" philosophy beyond all acceptable limits. Even more worrying to the government was the fact that many were members of the party, supposedly the guardians of public morality. In fact, economic reforms coupled with unashamed acquisitiveness had produced rampant corruption at every level of society.

A distinction has to be made between small-scale opportunism which enables ordinary Chinese to by-pass the restraints imposed on them by the vast bureaucracy, and the corruption of officials who exploit their positions for personal gain. Almost everyone bends the system a little, angling for small and usually legal advantages by "taking the back door". People take the back door to obtain the goods and services that are not sufficiently available through ordinary channels. A writer from Fuzhou described it as "an informal system for bartering and redistributing food and a few necessities of life. If you have a surplus of any commodity, then you head for the back door to get extra meat, more coal or whatever you want to bargain for."

Most back-door exchanges are based on the old Chinese custom of *guanxi*— the assiduous cultivation of personal connections among relatives, friends and colleagues. During the Cultural Revolution, for example, a nurse in

6

Peking found a way to avoid having her teenage son shipped off with squads of his contemporaries to dig ditches in the countryside. A special skill could bring exemption; to provide him with the necessary skill, the nurse persuaded a neighbour, a famous pianist, to give her son private lessons, although such individual tuition is a rarity in China. The nurse was later able to return the favour. When the pianist's mother became ill, the nurse arranged to have the woman admitted to a good hospital.

Certain occupations are valued because they give people a special opportunity to use the back door. Drivers, shop clerks and doctors are considered so fortunate that their jobs are referred to as the "three treasures". Because there are so few privately owned motor vehicles, drivers of trucks, buses and official cars have unique mobility. They get around to where the best back-door deals can be found; on Sunday a truck or car driver can put the vehicle to his own use—for pleasure or for rent. Clerks in department stores can buy scarce items such as radios and clothing before they reach the shelves. The goods can then be used to open other back doors.

Doctors are in a particularly advantageous position. They can barter medicines, sign certificates attesting that a patient is too sick to work, or literally let in through the back door of the surgery people who want to avoid long queues at public clinics. In exchange, the doctors can expect special courtesies from the local tailor or a choice table at a favourite restaurant.

The back door is considered a normal part of life by most Chinese. With the easing of economic restraints, however, more blatant, anti-social forms of sharp practice emerged. Free market traders took to storing goods until a shortage pushed prices up to many times the pre-shortage price. Meat condemned by the state as unfit for human consumption was siphoned to the market by the back door and sold to the unsuspecting public. State-subsidized products intended for sale at fixed prices were diverted on to the open market, at much higher prices.

Foreign companies in China have had to come to terms with local malpractices. A Chinese American co-owner of an hotel in Sichuan described a typical piece of underhand dealing involving customs agents. "The law says customs can take up to 10 per cent of an imported shipment of perishable items to test for disease," he explained. Rather than risk incurring delay and spoilage, hotel owners regularly pay off customs officials with "free samples". Foreign businessmen who remembered when an agreement could be sealed with a handshake, now found that the Chinese had no hesitation in breaking a contract if, for example, a commodity price changed.

An epidemic of the "red-eyed disease"—envy—swept China as it began to divide into a society of haves and have nots. Older people spoke yearningly about the good old days under Mao. Public contempt and anger grew, focused not so much against the hard-eyed speculators, as on the party officials who turned a blind eye to the corruption or actively participated in it, abusing their power by demanding bribes in return for contracts, by evading taxes, and by appointing family and friends to good schools and jobs. As Deng Xiaoping said, quoting an old Chinese saying, "When someone gets to the top, even his dogs and chickens get there too."

In the past, party members were virtually immune from prosecution unless they were accused of political crimes. Reluctant to investigate internal misdeeds, officials pursued their enquiries half-heartedly, as if "trying to catch a sparrow with their eyes closed". In one of the most blatant examples of the party protecting its own, a CCP secretary who was also a senior army officer escaped with nothing more than a salary cut and the loss of his official posts after being found guilty of misappropriating funds totalling 34 million yuan. He even kept his party membership. Six subordinate cadres did receive heavier punishments—in inverse proportion to their ranks. As another ancient Chinese adage puts it: "Punishments do not reach up to the lords."

Worried about the negative image of Chinese corruption, and disconcerted by the growing public disillusionment with the party, Deng ordered a campaign against official wrongdoers in 1988. But since many of the worst offenders occupied important positions in the party hierarchy, few Chinese expected the investigations to throw up more than a handful of scapegoats. In fact, 1988 saw the rehabilitation of Lei Yu, a party secretary who had been at the centre of a scandal in 1985. As economic overlord of the island of Hainan, Lei Yu had imported 79,000 foreign vehicles, 347,000 TV sets and 45,000 motorcycles for illegal resale at huge profits on the mainland. To oil the wheels of local officialdom, he had made pay-offs totalling one million yuan. Three years after, Lei Yu was appointed vice-mayor of Canton; the party, paying tribute to his business acumen, said that he was "receptive to new things" and "enjoys considerable prestige among cadres and people".

Not every party member is a follower of Mammon, of course, and not every official subverts the system for his own ends. Wu Baohua, party secretary in a village 500 kilometres south of Peking, is in many ways a communist of the old school, controlling most aspects of community life but exercising his authority for the people's good. When the local ice-cream factory failed to provide sufficient income, Wu had it converted into a cotton-fabric factory in six months. Faced with a drought, Wu organized a work gang of 4,000 Chinese, including himself, to dig a three-kilometre-long irrigation ditch from the Yellow River to the threatened fields. It was finished in 12 hours.

An unashamed admirer of Mao, who still commands from many Chinese a respect bordering on reverence, Wu has one of the former leader's sayings painted on a wall in his village: PREPARE FOR WAR, PREPARE FOR NATURAL DISASTER, SERVE THE PEOPLE. The slogan has a dated feel, and the last injunction, the motto of the PLA, has a hollow ring after the army's brutal suppression of the Tiananmen Square protestors in June, 1989. But Wu insists there is nothing wrong with the words. "We should use more of what Mao taught. His themes were self-reliance and sacrifice. I say to our leaders, more of that and less riding around in fancy cars."

"What we have today is a lot of talk about ending corruption and nepotism," Wu continues. "But unless we finally get serious about such things, we will never build our New China. We will watch Chinese on the outside rise because of their industry and intellect. We will never catch up."

A Shanghai hoarding advertising a Japanese-made wrist watch in Chinese and English is one of many that were put up in major cities during the late 1970s. It signalled a new emphasis on consumer goods and on modern marketing techniques.

AN EXECUTIVE'S FRUGAL LIFE

Photographs by Marc Riboud

"We have abolished class," a Chinese recently told a visitor, "but not rank." This fine distinction is exemplified by the lifestyle of Wang Yongcai *(right)*, manager of a vegetable-distribution depot in the Chongwen district of Peking. Wang supervises about 2,000 employees, holding a job equivalent to that of a high executive in the West. The personal lives of such "responsible persons" are not often revealed to foreigners, and the photographs on these and the following pages give a rare glimpse of a well-off Chinese family.

In many ways Wang and the members of his family—wife, daughter, son and daughter-in-law—belong to the same class as ordinary labourers; all five of them hold full-time jobs. Wang, like the workers under his supervision, dresses in blue workclothes, shares a plain workplace, and goes home to a small flat that is crowded with children and relatives.

Wang's managerial rank, however, is evident from such details as his use of a state-owned car, a luxury unavailable to most workers. "All people in China may look alike," noted a Chinese scientist, "but they are not. The differences are narrow, but for that reason are all the more keenly felt."

Wang Yongcai (*far right*) and his assistant wear overcoats—of obviously fine tailoring—against the chill of a cold storage room that is packed with overflowing baskets of onions, brought to the depot from farm areas around Peking for daily delivery to a distributor in the city.

Wang heads for his office from his chauffeur-driven white car, a luxury meant for official business. He usually bicycles between home and office.

During a weekly staff meeting, Wang *(second from right)* and 10 of his top assistants, all bareheaded, trade ideas with cap-wearing transportation chiefs. As at many conferences in China, tea and cigarettes are provided.

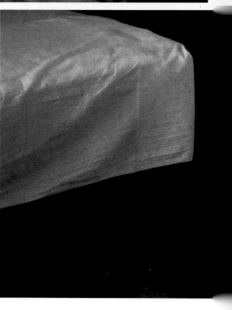

Wang washes up before the lunch break at an old-fashioned wash basin in the corner of his office.

Wang shares his office with his
assistant—although Wang's desk has
more drawers. The concrete-floored
room contains, in addition to the
wash basin, a coal stove and a cot for
the customary two-hour rest period.

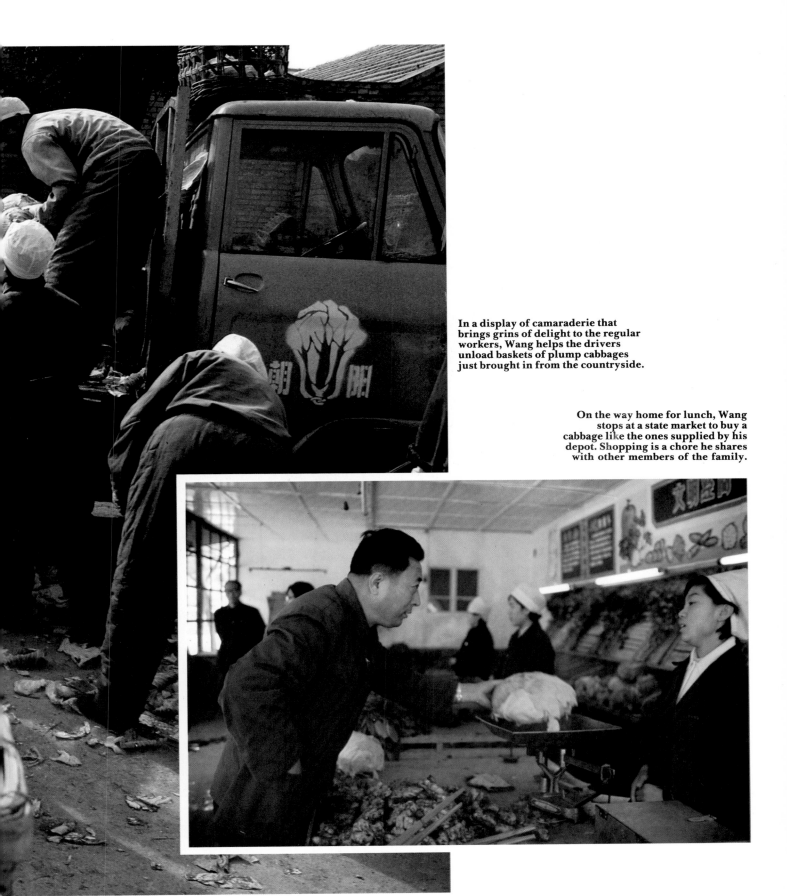

In a display of camaraderie that brings grins of delight to the regular workers, Wang helps the drivers unload baskets of plump cabbages just brought in from the countryside.

On the way home for lunch, Wang stops at a state market to buy a cabbage like the ones supplied by his depot. Shopping is a chore he shares with other members of the family.

139

AT HOME, LUNCH PREPARED BY FATHER

A steamer and a wok bubble on the Wangs' two-burner gas stove. It is in a small but separate kitchen, which is a luxury in Chinese flats. The bathroom, shared with neighbours in the building, is located in the hall.

Like many other men at all levels of Chinese society, Wang shares in the cooking and other housework. His culinary talents are exhibited as *(top to bottom)* he seasons, stirs and serves the family lunch, assisted by his daughter, son and daughter-in-law.

Wang and his wife *(second from right)* join younger family members in a meal of cabbage soup and vegetable and meat dishes that are eaten over steamed bread. In the background are neatly folded blankets; this main room also holds the parents' bed.

In their small bedroom, the son and his wife listen to music from a made-in-Shanghai cassette player on top of the tall chest. On the bureau are a clock and studio photographs of their wedding. The unmarried daughter has a tiny bedroom of her own.

143

A junk built to a design more than a
thousand years old carries freight into
the skyscraper-rimmed harbour of
Hong Kong. The British crown colony,
1,033 square kilometres surrounded by
the People's Republic of China, is
home to five million Chinese.

AN ETHNIC EMPIRE OVERSEAS

Beyond the borders of the People's Republic there is yet another China. It is a community that knows no boundaries, an ethnic empire that circles the globe. Nearly everywhere its people have preserved their special identity, hewing to traditional customs, language, festivals and foods. Wherever they have settled, they have proved remarkably adaptable, industrious and enterprising. In one region, South-East Asia, they have become a powerful, even dominant economic force.

Somewhat less than half the people constituting this ethnic empire call themselves *huaqiao*—literally, "Chinese resting on a journey"; the popular translation is "sojourners". By nearly everyone else they are referred to as Overseas Chinese. A slightly larger number of ethnic Chinese are *tongbao*, "compatriots", who make up the populations of Hong Kong and Taiwan. Some 40 million sojourners and compatriots live around the world, about 4 per cent of the population of the People's Republic—but important to it and to their homes far beyond their numbers. Of the more than 15 million sojourners, all but about a million are in South-East Asia, called in Chinese the *Nanyang* (the "south ocean"). They send some £75 million a year to relatives in the People's Republic; business deals between the PRC and companies run by sojourners pump three billion pounds a year in much-needed cash into Peking coffers.

Although the Overseas Chinese style themselves sojourners, 85 per cent of them were not born in mainland China but abroad. Few today have any expectation of ever returning to live in their ancestral homeland. In the 1950s and 1960s, some 500,000, most of them driven from their adopted countries by spates of anti-Chinese discrimination, did make such a return journey; but many of them—spurred by the excesses of the Cultural Revolution—swiftly departed again.

Although the *huaqiao* amount to only 6 per cent of the total population of South-East Asia, their influence on the economies (if not the politics) of the host countries is strikingly disproportionate. Through family networks resembling multinational corporations, they have amassed wealth estimated at £30 billion, some £8 billion of it invested in South-East Asian nations. One of the emigrants, Singapore banker Wong Nang Jang, summed up their importance when he said, "The Chinese are the common denominator of Asian business." It is a fact of life in much of South-East Asia that economic activity virtually ceases during the Chinese New Year holidays.

The economic power of the Overseas Chinese did not become dominant until the middle of the 20th century, although territorial adventurism had lured some Chinese beyond their country's borders as early as the third century B.C., when Shi Huang Di, the first

7

Emperor of the Qin Dynasty, conquered what is now Vietnam. About 1,500 years later, Kublai Khan sent a fleet with 20,000 men as far south as Java. The Khan's voyage of conquest proved to be a failure, but some men stayed behind to become settlers. And in the 15th century, Zheng He's famous expeditions *(Chapter 4)* ferried more Chinese to Cambodia, Siam, Sumatra, Ceylon and even to Persia and Africa.

The great majority of the Overseas Chinese, however, emigrated during the latter half of the 19th century and the first half of the 20th, spurred to leave by the same forces that simultaneously instigated mass emigration from Europe: political turmoil and hard times at home, the lure of opportunities in the rapid growth of industry and commerce abroad. Westerners were expanding commercial empires in Asia, while the United States looked for cheap, efficient labour.

By the hundreds of thousands, young Chinese men signed labour contracts. Ships carried these indentured "coolies" (from *kuli*, "hirelings", in the Indian language called Tamil) to Malaya to work in rubber plantations, to the Philippines to labour in gold mines, to Java and the United States to build railways. Others ended up in Canada, Brazil and Europe. But by far the largest numbers were transported to South-East Asia. In 1927, at the height of the outflowing tide, Singapore alone attracted 360,000 Chinese from the mainland. The Japanese invasion of China in 1937 hastened the exodus, as did the post-World War II struggle between the forces of Chiang Kai-shek and Mao Tse-tung.

Most of the early emigrants hoped to make their fortunes abroad and then return to China. Some did, each one jealously guarding a chest with personal belongings and hard-won silver coins. A typical picture of such *huaqiao* is evoked in Joseph Conrad's *Typhoon*.

The Nan-Shan was on her way from the southward to the treaty port of Fu-chau, with some cargo in her lower holds, and two hundred Chinese coolies returning to their village homes in the province of Fo-kien, after a few years of work in various tropical colonies. . . . The fore-deck, packed with Chinamen, was full of sombre clothing, yellow faces, and pigtails, sprinkled over with a good many naked shoulders, for there was no wind, and the heat was close. The coolies lounged, talked, smoked, or stared over the rail; some, drawing water over the side, sluiced each other; a few slept on hatches, while several small parties of six sat on their heels surrounding iron trays with plates of rice and tiny teacups; and every single Celestial of them was carrying with him all he had in the world—a wooden chest with a ringing lock and brass on the corners, containing the savings of his labours; some clothes of ceremony, sticks of incense, a little opium maybe, bits of nameless rubbish of conventional value, and a small hoard of silver dollars, toiled for in coal lighters, won in gambling houses or in petty trading, grubbed out of the earth, sweated out in mines, on railway lines, in deadly jungle, under heavy burdens—amassed patiently, guarded with care, cherished fiercely.

The typhoon that nearly sinks the ship *Nan-Shan* causes pandemonium below deck when the sliding chests burst and their owners, fighting for their scattering silver coins, tangle in a slashing, clawing mass that is rolled from side to side by the labouring ship. (The captain, once the storm is over, solves the dilemma by scooping up all the money and dividing it equally.)

This was the "piggy" (for "pigtail") trade of the 19th century. Most of the coolies had hardly reached home when they signed themselves out again. Each time, fewer came back. Virtually all of them still continued to believe that one day they would go home again. But gradually they became accustomed to life abroad, and the dreams of ancestral villages receded.

Wherever they settled, the sojourners earned success. In Brazil, Sheunming Ling developed one of the country's largest soy bean processing companies during the 1950s. From Switzerland, Michael Chu directs restaurants and hotels in half a dozen European countries. In the Philippines, the Cojuangco family controls two banks, large sugar plantations and a telephone company. In Thailand, Chin Sophonpanich is president and Jan Siriwongse is vice president of the Bangkok Bank, the largest Asian bank outside Japan. In the United States, three physicists of Chinese ancestry have won Nobel Prizes—Chen-ning Yang and Tsung-dao Lee in 1957, and Samuel C. C. Ting in 1976. In Australia, Tom Ah Chee is the millionaire owner of a chain of supermarkets.

Such success has been won in spite of difficult obstacles. During the 19th and early 20th century, the *huaqiao* were discriminated against, treated as second-class citizens or denied citizenship. When they achieved prosperity, it was envied and resented. In South-East Asia, where they were most numerous and most influential, anti-Chinese feeling was most intense. It reached a crescendo after World War II, when old colonial empires broke up. Once they had independence, the native peoples moved to wrest economic and political power from the Chinese with restrictive laws—or by more coercive means.

Anxious faces are mirrored in a display of the Hang Seng Index of the Hong Kong stock market. Hong Kong, a world financial centre, is noted for high-flying speculation. In one 15-month period, the index jumped from 347 to 1775, then fell to 189.

In 1962, Burma decided it would nationalize nearly all of its agriculture and industry, in which the nearly 400,000 resident Chinese had invested £50 million. Most of the sojourners left and went to other Asian countries.

Beginning in 1954, the Philippines surrounded commerce with legal restrictions aimed at the Chinese, but left enough loopholes to permit 500,000 *huaqiao* to prosper. Chinese shop signs are banned in Manila, but sections of the city are plastered with them; the shop owners simply pay an agreed-upon consideration to the policemen on the beat. In many cases, Filipinos serve as fronts, owning businesses the Chinese continue to manage. Often the front has been a Filipino woman with whom the Chinese businessman lives; if they were married, she too would be denied the right to own a business. The practice has been so widespread that by one estimate more than half the Chinese sojourners living in Manila have illegitimate children.

As stringent as the alien laws are in the Philippines, the Chinese there have not suffered in modern times from organized violence. They have not been so fortunate elsewhere. Numbers of Chinese were among the several million killed during the late 1970s by the regime of Pol Pot in Cambodia (today called Kampuchea). And sporadic violence set ethnic Chinese against indigenous groups in Malaya. When the Federation of Malaysia was founded in 1963, the sojourners nearly equalled the native population, 3.6 million Chinese to 4.5 million Malays, and the Chinese controlled 85 per cent of the retail trade, much of the nation's banking and perhaps one fourth of its export-import business. With the Chinese predominant in business, the Malays were determined to exclude them from the country's politics—which the Chinese naturally resented. The mutual antagonism that resulted was expressed in a bitter exchange between a wealthy Chinese merchant and a Malay government officer. "If it weren't for the Chinese," the merchant sneered, "you Malays would be sitting on the floor without tables and chairs." The Malay shot back, "If I knew I

7

could get every damned Chinaman out of the country, I would willingly go back to sitting on the floor.''

This resentment had been exacerbated by the activities of Communist insurgents—most of them Chinese and presumably supported by Peking—raising suspicions of subversion by Chinese residents. A power struggle between the sojourners and Malays erupted when, in a bitterly contested election in 1969, the Chinese minority mobilized enough votes to challenge the Malay control of Parliament. Three days later, Malays, armed with guns, knives and sharpened bamboo poles, rioted in the streets of the capital, Kuala Lumpur. One mob dragged a Chinese man from his car, set fire to it and then thrust the screaming victim back into the flaming vehicle.

The official body count in that rioting was 196, but the corpses had been shovelled into mass graves and, as one grave-digger admitted, "it was not always easy to know how many there were. The bodies had been cut into so many pieces." Western reporters esti-

mated the dead at between 1,500 and 2,000, most of them *huaqiao*.

But the bloodiest massacres occurred in 1965 in Indonesia, where the Overseas Chinese made up less than 4 per cent of the population but controlled the nation's commerce and a large part of its agriculture: a fifth of all farms were owned by the Chinese. Indonesian resentment of this economic power was aggravated by political suspicions during the mid-1960s when local Communists—presumably backed by the PRC—tried to take over the government. The attempted coup was crushed, and in its wake the government exacted a dreadful retribution from the *huaqiao*, Communists and non-Communists alike. Soldiers and vigilantes swept through the towns and villages, slaughtering any Chinese they found.

Perhaps the worst violence took place in Kalimantan—the Indonesian part of the island of Borneo—where headhunting Dyak tribesmen, encouraged by officials, burnt the villages of Chinese traders, trapping their victims

inside their homes. Any Chinese who ran from the blazing buildings were cut down and dismembered on the spot. Chinese refugees who left the countryside and sought the safety of the coastal cities were barracked in pestilence-ridden warehouses and systematically starved; thousands of these refugees died of cholera and dysentery.

Before the roving squads of assassins were through, some 300,000 "Communist supporters", most of them Chinese, had been killed. Sections of Jakarta's Chinatown were levelled. More than 200,000 surviving sojourners fled for their lives.

But many remained, and gradually the Indonesian government realized that the country might go bankrupt without its Overseas Chinese. Although some restrictive laws remained, they were largely ignored, and thousands of refugees returned. Two who fled and came back were banker Wee Mon-Cheng and his cousin, who had taken refuge in Singapore, where they had set up a company to distribute Dutch chocolates. As soon as the worst of the anti-Chinese actions had abated in Indonesia, Wee and his cousin built a chocolate factory there. "Chinese money," Wee explained, "moves to where the sun is shining."

The Chinese have made money grow phenomenally under the Asian sun despite discrimination and murderous hostility—in part by incessant toil, in part through their business acumen and in part simply because they help one another at every turn. They are bound together, first of all, by the Chinese heritage that they share, with its emphasis on family and village ties. Chinese who have roots in the same regions—and who speak the same dialect—are likely to be related and

KEY JOBS FOR SOJOURNERS

Despite South-East Asian efforts to limit the power of ethnic Chinese, they make up influential percentages *(table, below)* of key occupations in many countries.

	Thailand	The Philippines	Malaysia	Indonesia
Professions	1.59	40.0		1.5
Commerce and finance	50.84	41.0	24.0	36.6
Industry and handicraft	19.41	11.0	24.0	20.0
Agriculture	1.19		29.0	30.9
Unskilled	17.21	8.0	18.0	7.7

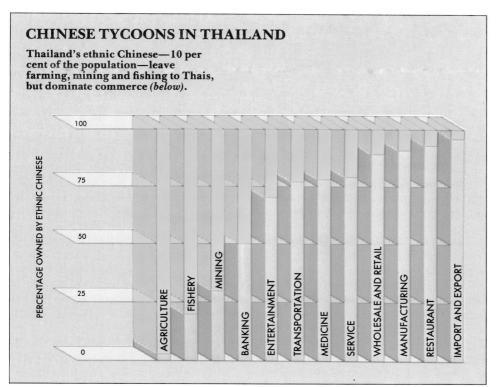

CHINESE TYCOONS IN THAILAND

Thailand's ethnic Chinese—10 per cent of the population—leave farming, mining and fishing to Thais, but dominate commerce (below).

PERCENTAGE OWNED BY ETHNIC CHINESE

100
75
50
25
0

AGRICULTURE
FISHERY
MINING
BANKING
ENTERTAINMENT
TRANSPORTATION
MEDICINE
SERVICE
WHOLESALE AND RETAIL
MANUFACTURING
RESTAURANT
IMPORT AND EXPORT

tend to be in the same businesses. "If you want a partner in Indonesia," explained one Singapore trader, "you work from the grass roots, looking for people like yourself, people in the clan. When you get cheated, it's better to get cheated by someone you know."

In Indonesia, immigrants from Fujian—the largest group—run rubber and plastics industries, the copra and coffee businesses, and textile factories. They also manufacture most of Jakarta's 150,000 pedi-taxis (which, significantly, are pedalled by Indonesians). The Cantonese and those speaking the Hakka dialect manage timber mills and rice-milling companies or own bakeries, tailor shops, furniture stores and restaurants. Smaller contingents of Jiangsu and Zhejiang immigrants specialize in clocks and watches, optical supplies and books. The Hubei Chinese are the dentists.

In Thailand, those speaking the Teo-chiu dialect, which is native to Shantou and Chaozhou, are exporters

and importers, and they also manage firms that are engaged in publishing and entertainment, shipping and finance. The Cantonese concentrate on construction, printing and the sugar industry. Chinese with roots in Hainan run hotels and chemist's shops.

Overseas Chinese with the same surnames, such as Zhu or Tan, also cleave together as if related. Most are not; there are only some 200 Chinese surnames among a billion people. Nevertheless, people with the same surname consider themselves of the same clan; in most South-East Asian cities, Chinese bearing like names have formed mutual-aid societies. Every member feels honour-bound to help all other members as if they were blood relatives. Even in Thailand, where the Chinese have assimilated more than anywhere else and have long intermarried with Thais (including the Royal Family of this enduring monarchy), the *huaqiao* retain their clan connections. There are more than 350 associ-

ations of one kind or another; in the clubhouses, members hold weddings and other festivities and collect funds to aid distressed clansmen.

The *huaqiao* in Thailand also preserve many customs and ways of life that give solidarity to Chinese communities everywhere. The traditional Chinese respect for age still rules, and many octogenarians run industrial empires. Offices still resound to the click of the abacus, and the clack of mah-jong tiles accompanies complicated deals made in teahouses. Few contracts are written, since among these Chinese entrepreneurs a person's word is his bond. The only paper present while such deals are made is the wrapping round the chicken at lunch.

Chinese families often live at the back of their shops or on the floors above, even in the most modern of office buildings. The family is an economic unit: everyone works in the store. One result is that *huaqiao* children learn commerce early and are better prepared for the business world than the Thai youngsters, who in any case disdain trade for government careers.

Many of Bangkok's Chinese are concentrated in what amounts to a Chinatown—the old Sempeng commercial district. It is an area of narrow lanes clotted with stores offering traditional Chinese goods: paper lanterns, toy shrines that are believed to bring their purchasers good fortune, and ancient herbal remedies, (said to delay ageing and promote sexual prowess) such as ginseng root and powdered deerhorn. Other shops sell Chinese musical instruments, including the poetically named moon guitar.

Chinese restaurants also abound in their area, some luxurious, some merely small eating-houses offering

7

only a few dishes. There are even itinerant restaurants—ambulatory chefs who carry small stoves through the streets on the end of poles, which are balanced at the other end by cupboards full of ingredients. They will squat down and prepare a snack at a moment's notice for businessmen during the evening rush hour or for Chinese longshoremen working the docks and rice boats on Thailand's great watery life line, the Chao Phya River.

Such enclaves of Chinese lifestyle, conspicuous in the predominating indigenous culture, exist almost everywhere. In Singapore, Taiwan and Hong Kong, however, the indigenous culture itself is Chinese, for these places are inhabited and controlled largely by Chinese. Powerful centres of trade and industry, they are also the most important—economically and politically—to the People's Republic.

Singapore, the world's third largest port, is the hub for much of the Asia-wide business of the Overseas Chinese, exporting goods worth some £10 billion annually. It handles nearly 80 per cent of Malaysia's and Indonesia's exports and imports. There are no mines or oil wells, but it has the world's third largest refinery complex—more than 22.5 million tonnes of petroleum products annually—and it is the principal centre of the rubber and tin markets. Singapore also is Asia's Switzerland, offering *huaqiao* investors numbered bank accounts and a tax-free sanctuary for "Asian dollar" (similar to Euro-dollar) deposits. Explained Finance Minister Hon Sui Sen, "I believe that money that suffers from ill treatment should be allowed a safe refuge just as persecuted religious minorities deserve a sanctuary."

In this sanctuary, the economy flourishes. Some 65 per cent of the population has achieved middle-class economic status; annual income is more than £1,250 per capita; and half of Singapore's children receive government-sponsored technical training to make their lot even better. Rags-to-riches stories abound in the executive suites along Shaenton Way.

Lien Ying-chow—born in a village in China's Guangdong province, an orphan at the age of nine and brought to Singapore when he was 12 by an uncle—started as a clerk, became an assistant office manager in his teens and founded his own firm when he was 21. At the time of the Japanese invasion of Singapore in 1941, he was already rich and was president of the Chinese Chamber of Commerce. He got out two days before the Japanese arrived and spent the war years in Australia, India and Chongqing, eventually returning to Singapore to found the huge Overseas Union Bank.

A more flamboyant figure in the tight little Singapore scene was Aw Boon Haw, who made his first fortune with a patent medicine that was called Tiger Balm ointment. Guaranteed to cure everything from rheumatism to bad breath, it was publicized with a spectacular amusement park in Singapore, Tiger Balm Gardens. With his profits from Tiger Balm, Aw launched a string of newspapers in Singapore, Hong Kong and elsewhere, and long before his death in 1954 he was famous for the size and the number of his philanthropic gifts. The family empire eventually grew to include a bank, a phonograph recording company and an insurance firm.

Perhaps even more colourful have been a pair of *huaqiao* brothers named Shaw, the undisputed moguls of the South-East Asian entertainment industry. The elder, Runme Shaw, emigrated from Shanghai to Singapore in the 1920s carrying a canvas suitcase containing the reels of three crude films he and his brother, Run Run Shaw, had shot in China. They swiftly set up a successful international film business; by 1941, their films were being shown in 110 cinemas all over South-East Asia.

When the Japanese invaded Singapore, the Shaws calmly buried their multimillion-dollar fortune in a hole in the back garden of their home, fled to Hong Kong and waited for peace. Returning to Singapore after the war, they found their hiding place undisturbed and were shortly back at work in an 18-hectare studio complex in the Kowloon section of Hong Kong. By the 1970s, the Shaw brothers' film empire, with Run Run producing the films in Hong Kong and Runme managing distribution from his headquarters in Singapore, was making more films per year than all of Hollywood's studios put together.

Sir Run Run—he was knighted by the British in 1977—starts a new film every nine days. Most are sex and sword-play fantasies, so popular that an estimated quarter of a million people in South-East Asia and the Chinatowns of the United States and Europe watch a Shaw film every day. The films are dubbed in English, French, German and Italian, as well as half a dozen Chinese dialects, and to cope with the intricacies of Asian censorship, Sir Run Run makes three versions of every film. Japan, Europe and the United States are sent a "hot" version ("We go to the limit," says Sir Run Run). A "warm" version is shown in Hong Kong, and a "cold" one is sent to the cinemas in Singapore, Malaysia,

In Singapore—populated by 1.85 million Chinese—residents in flats hang their laundry on projecting bamboo poles. The practice, which is a by-product of recent urbanization, is common in many Asian cities.

In Nationalist Taiwan, a mother and child worship at a Buddhist temple. China has adherents of all the major schools of Buddhism, which are often mixed with indigenous religious ideas and beliefs.

The Hotel Peninsula (above) in Hong Kong is as elegant as it was in Victorian times. But patrons now are principally Overseas Chinese taipans who have won the city's rich trade from the British.

7

Thailand and the People's Republic. Asked which were his best films, he replied: "the ones that make money".

The Shaw brothers own or have controlling arrangements with more than 700 cinemas in South-East Asia as well as Los Angeles, San Francisco and Honolulu. Their holdings include office buildings, amusement parks, a bewildering variety of investments and their own bank. When Sir Run Run admitted to a personal fortune of "hundreds of millions of dollars" and was asked whether he meant U.S. dollars, he smiled. "Hong Kong or U.S.," he asked, "what does it matter?"

The Shaws' headquarters in Singapore is far removed from the People's Republic; Singapore is an independent republic of only 618 square kilometres on an island at the southern tip of the Malay Peninsula some 2,415 kilometres from the Chinese border. Not so far removed—in distance and in their relationship to the PRC—are two other centres of Chinese life, Hong Kong and Taiwan. Here, the inhabitants are not sojourning Overseas Chinese but compatriots.

Taiwan is also an island—35,960 square kilometres, 160 kilometres east of the mainland in the South China Sea. It has been controlled by the Chinese, Dutch, Spanish, Portuguese (who called it Formosa—"beautiful island") and, from 1895 to 1945, by the Japanese. But only after Chiang Kai-shek's government, defeated in the civil war, took refuge there in 1949 did Taiwan become a monument to entrepreneurial success.

Building on an infrastructure left behind by the Japanese, the Taiwanese established a combination of agricultural and industrial stability that rapidly transformed the island. Its exports of nearly every imaginable product brought the government some £2.5 billion in foreign currency during the 1970s. By the end of that decade, it was shipping annually some £1.2 billion worth of clothing and £750 million in plastics, as well as more than nine million transistor radios worth £200 million and almost six million televisions worth more than £250 million.

As a result of this lively trade, Taiwan's living standard is exceeded in Asia only by those of Singapore, Hong Kong and Japan. Virtually all the homes in Taiwan have electricity. TV aerials rise from the roofs of farmhouses. Cars clog downtown Taipei, while thousands of motor scooters buzz through the constant traffic jams.

Taiwan absorbed two million refugees in a short time after 1949, but over the years the major refuge for Chinese emigrants has been Hong Kong. A sliver—1,068 square kilometres—of wheeling, dealing and affluence tucked into the drab egalitarianism of the People's Republic on the south coast near Canton, Hong Kong has one of the world's best harbours and serves as a port connecting China to the outside world. It is a hub of international air travel, a financial centre and a powerhouse of industry, with cotton mills, shipyards, ironworks, sugar refineries and fisheries. Part-ceded, part-leased (at gunpoint) to Britain in the 19th century, Hong Kong will revert to China in 1997.

Hong Kong's population—5.7 million in 1989—is 98 per cent Chinese. The border with China has been a sieve for more than a century. Along the 40-kilometre, hilly boundary, Chinese climb the wire fence or push it down; some are caught by border guards, given a free meal and sent back in trucks. Other escapees come by water on rafts of flotsam, tyres or even plastic bags. Some have found an ingenious use for the free condoms issued by the Peking government: they inflate them to provide flotation for their rafts. One prospering Hong Kong enterprise is the "snake boat" business: high-powered smuggling craft, some of which are faster than the patrol vessels of the Hong Kong Marine Police. Snake boat operators, charging up to £500 per passenger, sometimes find the demand so great that they have to issue tickets.

On arrival, Chinese refugees simply apply for identity cards to become residents; the government has long realized that the alternative would be an underclass of illegal aliens forced to pay "protection" money to criminals to avoid betrayal to the authorities, and who would have to accept sweatshop wages from exploitive employers.

Hong Kong's *laissez-faire* atmosphere has enabled hundreds of such refugees to acquire enormous wealth. In the 1980s, the richest of them all was probably Li Kashing, whose net worth was assessed at U.S.$2.5 billion in 1987. Li Kashing made his first millions by manufacturing plastic toys and flowers in the 1950s and 1960s before moving into the property market. Emboldened by success, he then set about wresting economic sovereignty from the once-unquestioned control of the British. For a century the more enterprising Chinese had provided middle management for the great British trading concerns, but the major decisions had been made in the mahogany-panelled boardrooms of Jardine Matheson, Hutchinson Whampoa and similar giant "hongs", the long-established British commercial firms.

The Chinese had also run auxiliary firms, and often become rich "taipans" doing so, but until 1980 none had seized control of a hong.

In that year billionaire Sir Yeu-kong Pao, owner of a huge fleet of tankers and freighters, set his sights on buying a company commonly known simply as The Wharf, a complex of warehouses that handled most of the goods moving into and out of the port. Pao quietly bought up 20 per cent of the stock, then negotiated a huge loan from the Hong Kong and Shanghai Banking Corporation (of which he was deputy chairman) and swiftly purchased more shares, enough to take over The Wharf. Almost simultaneously, his friend Li Kashing, who sold "Sir Y.K." that first 20 per cent of The Wharf, used the profits from this transaction to buy Hutchinson Whampoa. Hutchinson is among Hong Kong's "big five", one of the world's major trans-shipping firms and a diamond in the business establishment crown.

Both deals sent shock waves through the British business community, partly because Li had recently been made a director of the China International Trust and Investment Corporation, an agency of the People's Republic. Since the initiation of China's open-door economic policy, a curious symbiotic relationship has developed between Hong Kong, one of the most brashly capitalistic territories on earth, and the communist mainland. In 1987, China was the third-largest foreign investor in Hong Kong's manufacturing sector, close behind Japan and well ahead of the U.K. In the same year, two thirds of total foreign investment in China came from Hong Kong.

By far the most impressive symbol of

Leaving Hong Kong behind them, Overseas Chinese carefully manoeuvre their bundles as they board a train en route to southern China. Some five million annually cross the border to the PRC, lugging gifts ranging from food to television sets.

7

these economic links is the PRC's Bank of China, at 315 metres the tallest building in Hong Kong. Nearly 200 Peking bank branches have sprouted in the colony. Peking's China Resources Co. has a huge warehouse to handle goods from the mainland, and China Merchants Steam Navigation Co., set up to transport them, operates from its own Hong Kong headquarters. The PRC also owns a huge shipyard on Tsing Yi Island, and a multi-million pound machine tool plant which employs Hong Kong companies to market its lathes and milling equipment in South-East Asia.

China Products, a retail chain of stores owned by the People's Republic, has sprinkled Hong Kong with shops; its flagship department store is one of the largest on the island, offering everything from peasant folkcrafts to mini-calculators. It is crowded with customers buying luxuries for their families in the People's Republic. These economic ties partially allayed fears in the colony when, in 1984, Britain and China concluded a Joint Agreement for the return of Hong Kong to the People's Republic in 1997. Peking offered further reassurance by promising a "one country, two systems" framework of government, guaranteeing the continuation of Hong Kong's capitalist economy for at least 50 years. Many leading businessmen, envisaging an expanded role for Hong Kong as the financial capital of the Far East, greeted the agreement with acclaim. But others, less optimistic about China's intentions, decided not to wait and see what the future might hold. In 1988 alone, some 40,000 people sought to leave Hong Kong.

Any wary optimism about life under Chinese rule was shattered by the Tiananmen Square massacre of June 1989. In the immediate aftermath, the stock market plunged more than 20 per cent, and up to a million people poured through the streets to vent their grief, anger and fear over the killings. In a city where the main business has always been business, people discovered a newfound political activism. Calls were made for greater democratization. For though Hong Kong is democratic in spirit, members of its legislature are mainly appointed and, under the Joint Agreement, no elected chief executive is envisaged until at least 15 years after the handover.

The obvious question was: would Britain go ahead and hand over Hong Kong to China as agreed? The answer, soon forthcoming, was "yes". In that case, the Hong Kong Chinese demanded a right of refuge in Britain for the colony's 3.25 million British passport holders—people born in Hong Kong. The U.K. government refused, but later agreed in principle to grant residence status to 50,000 families of key professionals who might otherwise leave the territory before 1997. Even this concession was vehemently criticized by China's leaders and by many British politicians. Meanwhile, the exodus of Hong Kong residents, mainly to Canada and Australia, accelerated.

The best hope—the only hope—for the territory's future is that its continued prosperity remains in the interests of China, which desperately needs foreign trade and investment. If China can halt Hong Kong's drain of talent by demonstrating that it will conform to accepted norms of conduct, then Hong Kong could yet play a role out of all proportion to its size in influencing the further development of the giant on its doorstep.

The glittering lights of the Kowloon and Victoria districts frame the deep-water harbour that has made Hong Kong one of the world's busiest ports.

ACKNOWLEDGEMENTS

The index for this book was prepared by Barbara L. Klein and revised by Susanne Atkin. For their help with this volume, the editors wish to thank the following: Dr. John Aird, Foreign Demographic Analysis Division, U.S. Bureau of the Census, Washington, D.C.; Oscar Chiang, *Time*, New York; Carma Hinton, Cambridge, Mass.; Alfreda Murck, Assistant Curator Administrator, The Metropolitan Museum of Art, New York; Julia Murray, Freer Gallery of Art, Smithsonian Institution, Washington, D.C.; The State Statistical Bureau, People's Republic of China; Suzanne G. Valenstein, Associate Curator, The Metropolitan Museum of Art, New York; Marsha Wagner, Columbia University, Department of East Asian Languages and Culture, New York; Dr. Yuan-li Wu, Hoover Institution, Stanford, California.

The editors are indebted to the following quoted sources: *Report from a Chinese Village* by Jan Myrdal by permission of Pantheon Books, a division of Random House. *In The People's Republic* by Orville Schell by permission of Random House, Inc. *China: Alive in the Bitter Sea* by Fox Butterfield by permission of Times Books/The New York Times Book Co., Inc.

PICTURE CREDITS

Credits from left to right are separated by semicolons, from top to bottom by dashes.

Cover: Thomas Nebbia from Woodfin Camp Associates. Front endpaper: Map by Lloyd K. Townsend, Maytown, Pennsylvania. Back endpaper: Map by B-C Graphics, Bethesda, Maryland; digitized by Creative Data, London.

1, 2: © Flag Research Center, Winchester, Massachusetts. **6, 7**: © Yann Layma from Fovea, Paris; charts by Smith King and Company, Inc., digitized by Fingerprint Graphics Ltd., London. **8, 9**: Maps by Smith King and Company, Inc.; © Galen Rowell, Albany, California, digitized by Creative Data, London. **10, 11**: © Marc Riboud, Paris; charts by Smith King and Company, Inc., digitized by Fingerprint Graphics Ltd., London. **12, 13**: Bruno Barbey from Magnum, Paris; charts by Smith King and Company, Inc., digitized by Fingerprint Graphics Ltd., London. **14, 15**: Bruno Barbey from Magnum, Paris. **17**: Collections Albert Kahn, Département des Hauts-de-Seine, Boulogne-Billancourt. **18**: Eve Arnold from Magnum, New York. **19**: Ben Schonzeit. **20**: Nik Wheeler, Los Angeles. **21**: Map by B-C Graphics, digitized by Creative Data, London. **22, 23**: Nik Wheeler. **24**: Richard D. Gordon, Philadelphia. **25**: Lowell Georgia, Arvada, California. **26**: Richard D. Gordon, Philadelphia. **28**: © Marc Riboud, Paris. **29**: © D.E. Cox, Click/Chicago, Ltd., 1979. **32-43**: Richard D. Gordon. **44-46**: Thomas Nebbia, Santa Monica, California. **47**: Map by B-C Graphics, digitized by Creative Data, London. **49**: © Michael Ruetz from Focus, Hamburg. **50, 51**: Burt Glinn from Magnum, New York. **52**: Richard D. Gordon, Philadelphia; Thomas and Gitte Nebbia, Santa Monica, California (2). **53**: © John Henebry Jr., Wilmette, Illinois; © Galen Rowell (2). **54**: David Thurston, London. **55**: © Kit Luce from Focus, Hamburg. **56, 57**: Richard D. Gordon. **58, 59**: © Galen Rowell. **60, 61**: Thomas Nebbia; Richard D. Gordon. **62, 63**: © Galen Rowell. **64, 65**: Thomas and Gitte Nebbia, **66, 67**: © Michael Ruetz from Focus, Hamburg. **68, 69**: Courtesy the Freer Gallery of Art, Smithsonian Institution, Washington, D.C. **71–76**: Marc Riboud, Paris. **79**: David Thurston, London. **80**: Richard D. Gordon. **82, 83**: Courtesy the Freer Gallery of Art, Smithsonian Institution, Washington, D.C.—Wan-go H.C. Weng, Lyme, New Hampshire; courtesy the Freer Gallery of Art, Smithsonian Institution, Washington, D.C. (2); The Metropolitan Museum of Art, Mr. and Mrs. Isaac D. Fletcher Collection, bequest of Isaac D. Fletcher, 1917. **84**: Peter Carmichael from ASPECT, London. **86, 87**: Museum of Fine Arts, Boston; courtesy The Cultural Relics Bureau, Beijing, and The Metropolitan Museum of Art, New York (2); The Nelson-Atkins Museum of Art, Kansas City, Missouri, gift of Mr. Earle Grant; The Nelson-Atkins Museum of Art, Kansas City, Missouri, gift of Mr. S. Yamanaka. **88**: Keystone View Company, New York, the Von Harringa Collection. **91**: Wan-go H.C. Weng. **92**: Courtesy the Freer Gallery of Art, Smithsonian Institution, Washington, D.C., except centre, Library of Congress, Washington, D.C. **93**: Thomas and Gitte Nebbia—Library of Royal Botanical Gardens, Kew, photographed by Eileen Tweedy; *Heck's Encyclopedia of Source Illustrations*, courtesy Library of Congress—Library of Congress; *March of Time*. **94**: Paul Dorsey for *Life*; © Flag Research Center, Winchester, Massachusetts; © Marc Riboud, Paris—Sovfoto, New York. **97**: Wan-go H.C. Weng. **98**: The British Library, London, photographed by Eileen Tweedy. **99**: Felice Beato, courtesy Chao-ying Fang. **100**: Bosshard from Black Star, New York. **102, 103**: Jack Wilkes for *Life*; Carl Mydans for *Life*. **104, 105**: Jack Birns for *Life*; Henri Cartier-Bresson from Magnum, Paris. **106, 107**: Jack Birns for *Life* (2); James Burke for *Life*. **108**: Grabet from Gamma-Liaison, New York. **110**: Chart by Smith King and Company, Inc., digitized by Creative Data, London. **111**: Henri Cartier-Bresson for *Life*. **113**: © Marc Riboud, Paris. **114**: Harry Redl from Black Star, New York. **116**: © D.E. Cox, 1979. **118**: © Stuart Franklin from Magnum, London. **120, 121**: © 1981 Larry Mulvehill from Photo Researchers, Inc., New York. **122**: Nik Wheeler. **123**: Chart by B-C Graphics, digitized by Creative Data, London. **127**: Bruno Barbey from Magnum, Paris. **130**: © Marc Riboud, Paris. **133**: Bruno Barbey from Magnum, Paris. **134–143**: Marc Riboud, Paris. **144, 145**: Alain McKenzie, Paris. **147**: © 1982 Robin Moyer from Black Star, New York. **148, 149**: Charts by Smith King and Company, Inc., digitized by Creative Data, London. **151**: © John Henebry Jr.; © Ira Lipsky from International Stock Photography Ltd., New York; © Robert Frerck from Odyssey Productions. **153**: Peter Carmichael from ASPECT, London. **154, 155**: © Robert Frerck from Odyssey Productions, Chicago.

BIBLIOGRAPHY

BOOKS

Alexander, Garth, *The Invisible China: The Overseas Chinese and the Policies of Southeastern Asia.* Macmillan, 1973.

Avedon, John F., *In Exile from the Land of the Snows.* Wisdom Publications, 1985.

Bailey, P.J., *China in the Twentieth Century.* Basil Blackwell, 1988.

Balzer-Hsu, Eileen, et al., *China Day by Day.* Yale University Press, 1974.

Baum, Richard, *China in Ferment.* Prentice-Hall, 1971.

Bennett, Gordon, *Huadong: The Story of a Chinese People's Commune.* Westview and William Heinemann, 1978.

Bernstein, Richard, *From the Center of the Earth.* Little, Brown, 1982.

Bianco, Lucien, *Origins of the Chinese Revolution 1915–1949.* Stanford University Press, 1971.

Bonavia, David, *The Chinese.* Allen Lane, 1981.

Bonavia, David, and Magnus Bartlett, *Tibet.* Thames & Hudson, 1981.

Buchanan, Keith, et al., *China.* Crown, 1980.

Bunge, Fredrica M., and Rinn-Sup Shinn, *China—A Country Study.* U.S. Government Printing Office, 1981.

Butterfield, Fox, *China—Alive in the Bitter Sea.* Hodder & Stoughton, 1983.

Carter, Thomas Francis, *The Intervention of Printing in China.* Ronald Press, 1955.

Chang, Raymond, and Margaret Scrogin Chang, *Speaking of Chinese.* André Deutsch, 1981.

Chen, Jack, *A Year in Upper Felicity.* Macmillan, 1973.

China Facts and Figures. Peking: Foreign Languages Press, 1982.

China: A General Survey. Peking: Foreign Languages Press, 1979.

Conrad, Joseph, *Typhoon.* William Heinemann, 1966.

Fairbank, John K., et al., *East Asia, Tradition and Transformation.* Houghton-Mifflin, 1973.

Fathers, Michael, and Andrew Higgins, *Tiananmen: The Rape of Peking.* Transworld Publishers, 1989.

Fong, Wen, ed., *The Great Bronze Age of China: An Exhibition from the People's Republic of China.* The Metropolitan Museum of Art, Alfred A. Knopf, 1980.

Fraser, John, *The Chinese: Portrait of a People.* Collins, 1981.

Frolic, Michael, *Mao's People.* Harvard University Press, 1980.

Gittings, John, *China Changes Face.* Oxford University Press, 1989.

Hinton, Harold C., *The People's Republic of China: A Handbook.* William Dawson, 1979.

Hook, Brian, ed., *The Cambridge Encyclopedia of China.* Cambridge University Press, 1982.

Hucker, Charles O., *China to 1850: A Short History.* Stanford University Press, 1978.

Journey into China. National Geographic Society, 1982.

Kaplan, Fredric M., and Julian M. Sobin, *Encyclopedia of China Today.* Macmillan, 1982.

Kingston, Maxine Hong, *China Men.* Picador Books, 1981.

Kratochvil, Paul, *The Chinese Language Today.* Hutchinson University Library, 1968.

Latham, Ronald, *The Travels of Marco Polo.* Abaris Books, 1982.

Latourette, Kenneth Scott, *The Chinese, Their History and Culture.* Macmillan, 1962.

Lee, Sherman E., and Wen Fong, *Streams and Mountains without an End.* Artibus Asiae, 1967.

Li, Dun J.:
The Ageless Chinese. Charles Scribner's Sons, 1971.
The Essence of Chinese Civilization. D. Van Nostrand, 1967.

Lin Yutang, *My Country and My People.* John Day, 1939.

Meisner, Maurice, *Mao's China.* Collier Macmillan, 1979.

Meskill, John T., *An Introduction to Chinese Civilization.* Heath, 1973.

Morton, W. Scott, *China, Its History and Culture.* McGraw-Hill, 1980.

Munsterberg, Hugo, *The Arts of China.* Charles E. Tuttle, 1972.

Mydal, Jan, *Report from a Chinese Village.* Vintage Books, 1965.

Mydans, Carl, and Michael Demarest, *China: A Visual Adventure.* Simon and Schuster, 1979.

Needham, Joseph, *Science and Civilization in China.* Vol. 4. Cambridge University Press, 1962.

Obata, Shigeyoshi, *The Works of Li Po, the Chinese Poet.* Paragon Books, 1965.

Pruitt, Ida, *A Daughter of Han.* Stanford University Press, 1967.

Rafferty, Kevin, *City on the Rocks: Hong Kong's Uncertain Future.* Viking, 1989.

Reischauer, Edwin, and John K. Fairbank, *East Asia, the Great Tradition.* George Allen & Unwin, 1961.

Rodzinski, Witold, *The People's Republic of China.* Fontana, 1989.

Schell, Orville, *In the People's Republic.* Victor Gollancz, 1978.

Schurmann, Franz, and Orville Schell, *Communist China.* Vintage Books, 1967.

Shawcross, William, *Kowtow!* Chatto & Windus, 1989.

Statistical Yearbook of China 1981. Peking: State Statistical Bureau, 1982.

Sullivan, Michael, *The Arts of China.* Sphere Books, 1973.

Tsao, Hsueh-chin, *Dream of the Red Chamber.* Anchor Books, 1958.

Waley, Arthur:
The Analects of Confucius. George Allen & Unwin, 1964.
An Introduction to the Study of Chinese Painting. Ernest Benn, 1958.
Translations from the Chinese. Alfred A. Knopf, 1941.

Wang, Gung-Hsing, *The Chinese Mind.* John Day, 1964.

Watson, Burton, *Early Chinese Literature.* Columbia University Press, 1962.

Weng, Wan-go, and Yang Boda, *The Palace Museum, Peking: Treasures of the Forbidden City.* Orbis, 1982.

Wright, Elizabeth, *The Chinese People Stand Up.* BBC Books, 1989.

Zhang Xinxin and Sang Ye, *Chinese Lives,* Penguin Books, 1989.

PERIODICALS

Allman, T.D., "Credit Cards and Calculators Come to Shangri-La." *Asia,* Jan./Feb. 1981.

"The Chinese Abroad." *Time,* Dec. 12, 1977.

Burton, Sandra, "Red-Letter Day." *Time,* Sept. 25, 1989.

Cohen, Jerome Alan, "Has Justice a Fairer Future in China?" *Asia,* Jan./Feb. 1979.

Domes, Jurgen, "New Policies in the Communes: Notes of Rural Societal Structures in China, 1976–1981." *Journal of Asian Studies,* Feb. 1982.

Eberhard, Wolfram, "Chinese Regional Stereotypes." *Asian Survey,* Dec. 1965.

Gonzales, Nancie L., "Organization of Work in China's Communes." *Science,* 218: 898–903, 1982.

Gore, Rick, "Journey to China's Far West." *National Geographic,* Mar. 1980.

Harding, Harry, "Reappraising the Cultural Revolution." *The Wilson Quarterly,* Autumn 1980.

Higgins, Andrew, "China 1989: The Year of the Revolution." *The Independent,* Dec. 27, 1989.

Hua Jueming, "The Mass Production of Iron Castings in Ancient China." *Scientific American,* Jan. 1983.

Karnow, Stanley, "The Crown Colony Coins a New Image." *Asia,* May/June 1982.

Kraar, Louis:
"Beijing's Overseas Chinese Connection." *Asia,* July/Aug. 1979.
"China's Drive for Capitalist Profits in Hong Kong." *Fortune,* May 21, 1971.
"The Wealth and Power of the Over-Seas Chinese." *Fortune,* Mar. 1971.

Kramer, Michael, "Free to Fly Inside the Cage." *Time,* Oct. 2, 1989.

Pannell, Clifton W., "Less Land for Chinese Farmers." *The Geographical Magazine,* June 1982.

Rowan, Roy, "China's Creeping Capitalism." *Fortune,* Dec. 28, 1981.

Rowell, Galen, "Nomads of China's West." *National Geographic,* Feb. 1982.

Schaller, George, "Pandas in the Wild." *National Geographic,* Dec. 1981.

Schell, Orville:
"Journey to the Tibetan Plateau." *Natural History Magazine,* Sept. 1982.
"Return to China's Curbside Capitalists." *Asia,* July/Aug. 1980.

Stewart, William, "Fear and Anger in Hong Kong." *Time,* June 19, 1989.

Weil, Martin, "China's Consuming Interests." *China Business Review,* Jan./Feb. 1982.

INDEX

Page numbers in italics refer to illustrations or illustrated text.

Typesetting by Tradespools Ltd., Somerset, England
Printed and bound by Artes Gráficas Toledo, S.A., Spain.

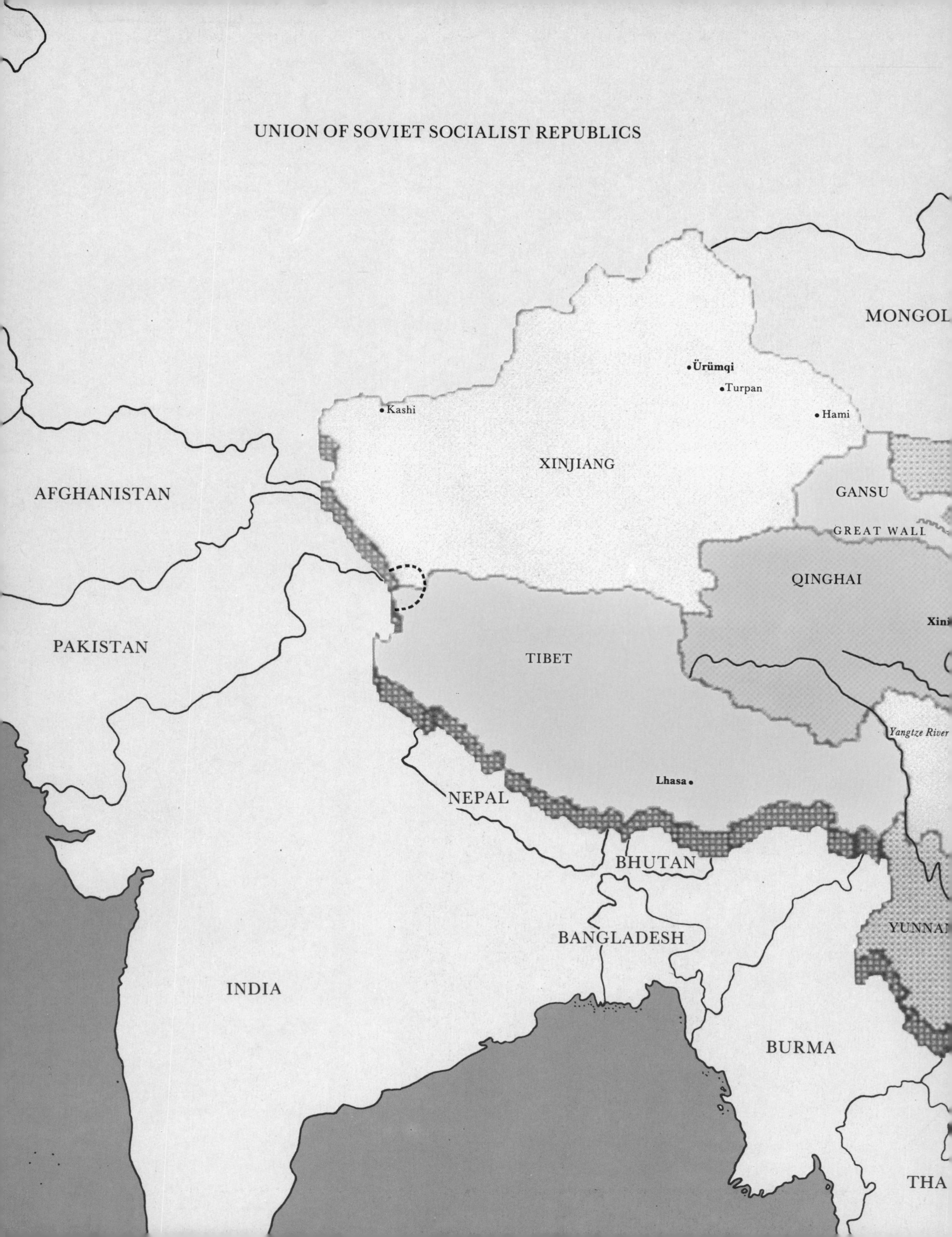

UNION OF SOVIET SOCIALIST REPUBLICS

MONGOL

• Ürümqi
• Turpan

• Hami

• Kashi

XINJIANG

GANSU

GREAT WALL

AFGHANISTAN

QINGHAI

Xin

PAKISTAN

TIBET

Yangtze River

NEPAL

Lhasa •

BHUTAN

BANGLADESH

YUNNA

INDIA

BURMA

THA